BASICS OF KEYBOARD THEORY

LEVEL 8

Fourth Edition

Julie McIntosh Johnson

J. Johnson Music Publications

5062 Siesta Lane
Yorba Linda, CA 92886
Phone: (714) 961-0257
Fax: (714) 242-9350
www.bktmusic.com
info@bktmusic.com

Fourth Edition ©2007, Julie McIntosh Johnson
Previous Editions ©1983, 1992, 1997, Julie McIntosh Johnson

Basics of Keyboard Theory, Level 8, Fourth Edition

Published by:

J. Johnson Music Publications
5062 Siesta Lane
Yorba Linda, CA 92886 U.S.A.
(714) 961-0257
www.bktmusic.com

All rights reserved. No part of this book may be reproduced or transmitted in any form or by any means, electronic or mechanical, including photocopying, recording, or by any information storage and retrieval system without written permission from the author, except for the inclusion of brief quotations in a review.

©2007 by Julie McIntosh Johnson. Revised.
Previous editions ©1983, 1992, and 1997, Julie McIntosh Johnson.
Printed in U.S.A.

Library of Congress Cataloging in Publication Data

Johnson, Julie Anne McIntosh
Basics of Keyboard Theory, Level 8, Fourth Edition

ISBN 10: 1-891757-08-3
ISBN 13: 978-1-891757-08-2

LC TX 4-721-496

Basics of Keyboard Theory, Level 1 corresponds with the MTAC Certificate of Merit™ Piano Syllabus. Certificate of Merit™ is an evaluation program of the Music Teachers' Association of California. Reference to 'Certificate of Merit™' (CM) does not imply endorsement by MTAC of this product.

TO THE TEACHER

Intended as a supplement to private or group music lessons, *Basics of Keyboard Theory, Level 8* presents basic theory concepts to the advanced music student. This level is to be used with the student who has had approximately eight to nine years of music lessons, and is playing piano literature at the level of Khachaturian's *Sonatina, 1959,* or Mozart's *Variations on Twinkle Twinkle Little Star*.

Basics of Keyboard Theory, Level 8 is divided into nineteen lessons, with two reviews, and a test at the end. Application of each theory concept is made to piano music of the student's level. Lessons may be combined with one another or divided into smaller sections, depending on the ability of the student. Whenever possible, it is helpful to demonstrate theory concepts on the keyboard, and apply them to the music the student is playing.

Learning music theory can be a very rewarding experience for the student when carefully applied to lessons. *Basics of Keyboard Theory, Level 8* is an important part of learning this valuable subject.

BASICS OF KEYBOARD THEORY
COMPUTER ACTIVITIES
by
Nancy Plourde
with
Julie McIntosh Johnson and Anita Yee Belansky

Colorful, exciting games that reinforce Basics of Keyboard Theory lessons!

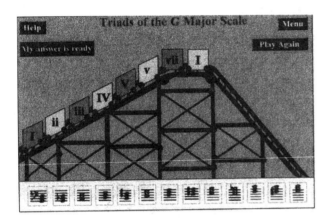
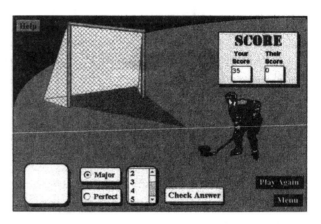

LEVELS PREPARATORY, 1, and 2: 30 GAMES, 10 PER LEVEL!
LEVELS 3 and 4: 20 GAMES, 10 PER LEVEL!
LEVELS 5 and 6: 20 GAMES, 10 PER LEVEL!
Corresponds with MTAC CM Syllabus & *Basics of Keyboard Theory* books, or may be used independently.

Download a free demo at www.pbjmusic.com

--Order Form---

Name_____
Address_____
City_____State_____Zip_____
Email_____Phone_____

Mail to: PBJ Music Publications
5062 Siesta Ln.
Yorba Linda, CA 92886
(714) 961-0257

Qty		Cost
_____	Levels Prep-II, Mac/PC: $49.95	_____
_____	Levels III-IV, Mac/PC: $39.95	_____
_____	Levels 5-6, PC only: $49.95	_____
	Sub Total:	_____
	Sales Tax (CA, AZ, TX residents)	_____
	Shipping:	$5.00
	Total:	_____

System Requirements
IBM or compatible: 486 33 MHz or higher, Windows 3.1, 95, 98, NT, or XP, or Vista, 8 MB RAM, 5 MB hard disk space, MIDI Soundcard, VGA monitor.
Mac: System 7 or greater, 8 MB RAM, 3 MB hard disk space, color monitor. OS X requires Classic Mode or Boot Camp.

TABLE OF CONTENTS

Lesson 1: Major and Minor Key Signatures..1

Lesson 2: Scales...13

Lesson 3: Intervals...21

Lesson 4: Diatonic and Chromatic Half Steps..25

Lesson 5: Major, Minor, Augmented, and Diminished Triads and Inversions.............................29

Lesson 6: Primary and Secondary Triads; Figured Bass..37

Lesson 7: Dominant and Diminished Seventh Chords...45

Lesson 8: The Secondary Dominant...51

Lesson 9: Authentic, Half, Plagal, and Deceptive Cadences; Chord Progressions......................57

Lesson 10: Modulation..67

Review: Terms Used in Lessons 1-10...73

Review: Lessons 1-10...75

Lesson 11: Time Signatures..83

Lesson 12: Signs and Terms..93

Lesson 13: Contrapuntal Techniques..105

Lesson 14: Homophonic and Polyphonic Textures..113

Lesson 15: Transposition...117

Lesson 16: The Four Periods of Music History; The Baroque Period; Kirnberger, Telemann, and Vivaldi..121

Lesson 17: The Classical Period; Clementi, Czerny, and Diabelli...129

Lesson 18: The Romantic Period; Field, Heller, and Mendelssohn...135

Lesson 19: The Contemporary Period; Britten, Poulenc, and Stravinsky..................................141

Review: Lessons 11-19...147

Review Test...155

Basics of Keyboard Theory is dedicated to my husband Rob, without whose love, support, help, and incredible patience, this series would not have been possible.

LESSON 1
MAJOR AND MINOR KEY SIGNATURES

The **KEY SIGNATURE** for a musical composition is found at the beginning of the piece, next to the clef signs.

The **KEY SIGNATURE** tells you two things:

1. The **key** or **tonality** of the music.

2. Which notes in the music are to receive sharps or flats.

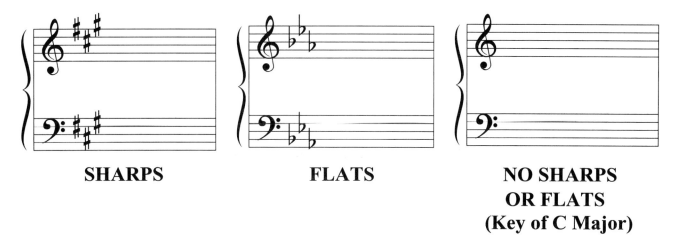

SHARPS **FLATS** **NO SHARPS OR FLATS** (Key of C Major)

If the key signature has <u>SHARPS</u>, they will be written in this order, on these lines and spaces. This is called the **ORDER OF SHARPS**.

THE ORDER OF SHARPS

A saying to help you remember this order is:

Fat Cats Go Down Alleys Eating Bologna

If a key signature has one sharp, it will be F♯. If a key signature has two sharps, they will be F♯ and C♯, etc.

To determine which Major key a group of sharps represents, find and name the last sharp (the sharp furthest to the right), then go up a half step from that sharp. The note which is a half step above the last sharp is the name of the Major key.

Three sharps: F♯, C♯, G♯

Last sharp is G♯

A half step above G♯ is A

Key of A Major

To determine which sharps are in a Major key, find the sharp which is a half step below the name of the key. Name all the sharps from the Order of Sharps up to and including that sharp.

Key of D Major

A half step below D is C♯

Name all sharps, from the Order of Sharps, up to and including C♯

F♯ and C♯

If a key signature has <u>FLATS</u>, they will be in the following order, written on these lines and spaces. This is called the **ORDER OF FLATS.**

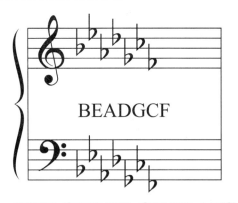

THE ORDER OF FLATS

The Order of Flats can be memorized this way:

BEAD Gum Candy Fruit

If a key signature has one flat, it will be B♭. If it has two flats, they will be B♭ and E♭, etc.

To determine which Major key a group of flats represents, simply name the next to last flat.

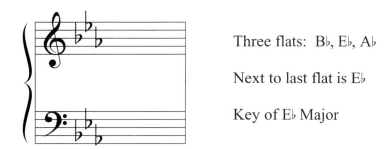

Three flats: B♭, E♭, A♭

Next to last flat is E♭

Key of E♭ Major

To determine which flats are needed for a given key, name all the flats from the Order of Flats up to and including the name of the key, then add one more.

Key of E♭ Major

Name all flats from the Order of Flats up to and including E♭, then add one more.

B♭, E♭, A♭

The key signature for F Major has to be memorized. It has one flat: B♭.

KEY SIGNATURE FOR F MAJOR

Major keys which have sharps will be named with a letter only, or a letter and a sharp (for example, G Major, D Major, F♯ Major).

Major keys which have flats will have a flat in their name (for example, B♭ Major, D♭ Major, E♭ Major).

The two exceptions to the above rules are F Major (one flat: B♭), and C Major (no sharps or flats).

1. Name these Major keys.

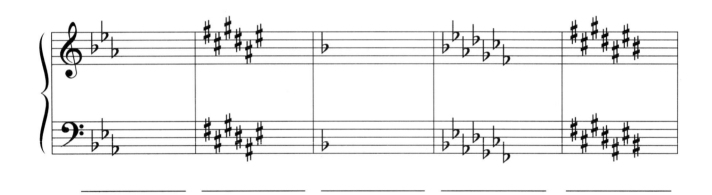

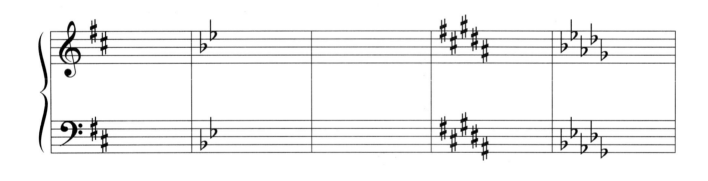

2. Write the key signatures for these Major keys.

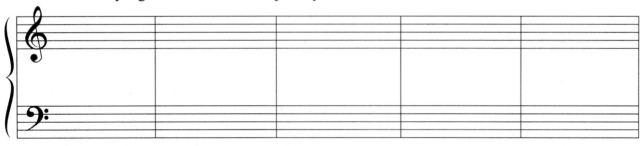

D Major   F♯ Major   A♭ Major   E Major   F Major

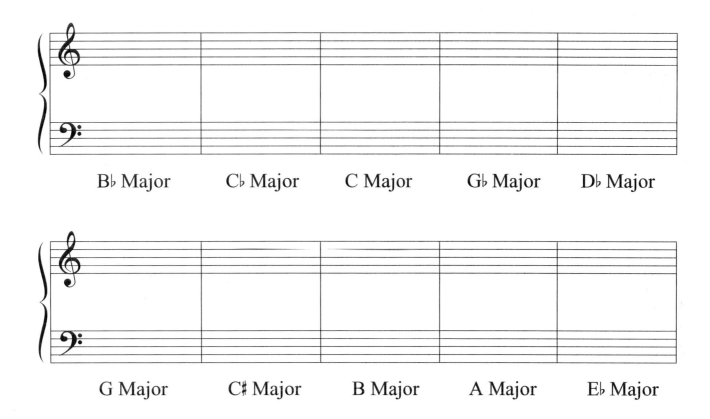

| Bb Major | Cb Major | C Major | Gb Major | Db Major |

| G Major | C# Major | B Major | A Major | Eb Major |

Many Major key signatures have **RELATIVE MINORS**. The relative minor is found by going down three half steps from the name of the Major key. Skip one letter between the names of the keys.

KEY SIGNATURE FOR D MAJOR
THREE HALF STEPS BELOW D IS B
KEY OF B MINOR

One way to determine whether a composition is in the Major or minor key is to look at the last note of the piece. It is usually the same as the name of the key. (For example, a piece which is in the key of e minor will probably end on E.) Also, look at the music to find the note around which the music appears to be centered. This should be the same as the name of the key.

3. Write the name of the relative minor for each of the following Major keys.

G Major   _____   A♭ Major   _____

E♭ Major   _____   A Major   _____

C Major   _____   E Major   _____

F Major   _____   D♭ Major   _____

B♭ Major   _____   G♭ Major   _____

D Major   _____   B Major   _____

4. Give the name of the relative Major for each of the following minor keys.

d minor   _____   g minor   _____

e minor   _____   b minor   _____

f minor   _____   c♯ minor   _____

c minor   _____   b♭ minor   _____

a minor   _____   e♭ minor   _____

f♯ minor   _____   g♯ minor   _____

5. Name these minor keys.

6. Write the key signatures for these minor keys. (Go up three half steps to find the relative Major, then write the key signature for that Major key.)

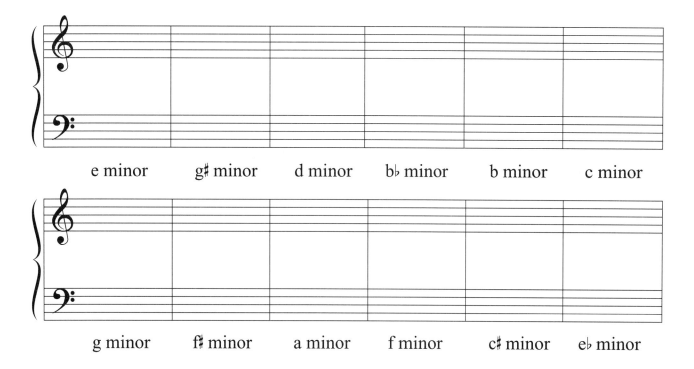

7. Give the name of the Major or minor key for each of the following musical examples.

a. From *Mazurka, Op. 67, No. 4,* by Chopin. _____

b. From *Bunte Blatter, Op. 99, No. III,* by Schumann. _____

c. From *Variations on Ah! vous dirai-je, Maman,* by Mozart. _____

d. From *La fille aux cheveux de lin,* by Debussy. _____

e. From *Waltz, Op. posth. 69, No. 1,* by Chopin. _____

f. From *Sonata, Op. 49, No. 1,* by Beethoven. _____

g. From *Invention No. 3* by J.S. Bach. _____

h. From *Kinderscenen, Op. 15, No. 6,* by Schumann. _____

8. Memorize these key signatures.

   C Major and a minor: no sharps or flats
   G Major and e minor: F♯
   D Major and b minor: F♯ and C♯
   A Major and f♯ minor: F♯, C♯, and G♯
   E Major and c♯ minor: F♯, C♯, G♯, and D♯
   B Major and g♯ minor: F♯, C♯, G♯, D♯, and A♯
   F♯ Major and d♯ minor: F♯, C♯, G♯, D♯, A♯, and E♯
   C♯ Major: F♯, C♯, G♯, D♯, A♯, E♯, and B♯
   F Major and d minor: B♭
   B♭ Major and g minor: B♭, and E♭
   E♭ Major and c minor: B♭, E♭, and A♭
   A♭ Major and f minor: B♭, E♭, A♭, and D♭
   D♭ Major and b♭ minor: B♭, E♭, A♭, D♭, and G♭
   G♭ Major and e♭ minor: B♭, E♭, A♭, D♭, G♭, and C♭
   C♭ Major and a♭ minor: B♭, E♭, A♭, D♭, G♭, C♭, and F♭

The **CIRCLE OF FIFTHS** (sometimes called the **Circle of Keys**) is a method of organizing the Major and minor keys so that when ascending by perfect fifths from key to key, one sharp is added to each new key. When the keys of B, F♯, and C♯ are reached, there is an enharmonic change (notes with the same pitch but different letter names, such as F♯ and G♭). Flats are then used, and as the keys ascend by perfect fifths, one flat is deleted from each key.

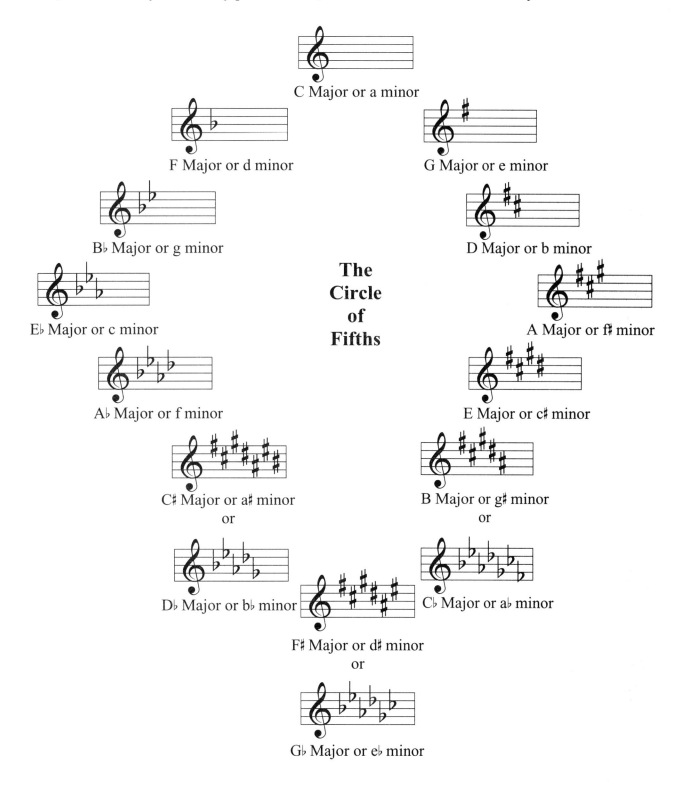

9. Fill in the Circle of Fifths (Circle of Keys) below. Include the Major and minor key names, enharmonic equivalents, and write each key signature on the staff.

LESSON 2
SCALES AND MODES

SCALES are made up of a series of notes, which are each a step apart. They begin and end with notes of the same letter name.

MAJOR SCALES contain eight notes, and have all the sharps or flats from the Major key signature with the same name. **IONIAN MODE** has the same pattern of whole and half steps as the major scale.

D MAJOR SCALE or IONIAN MODE ON D

NATURAL MINOR SCALES contain all the sharps or flats from the minor key signature with the same name. Example:d natural minor scale begins and ends with the note "D," and has B♭. **AEOLIAN MODE** has the same pattern of whole and half steps as the natural minor scale.

D NATURAL MINOR SCALE or AEOLIAN MODE

HARMONIC MINOR SCALES are created by raising the seventh note of the natural minor scale a half step. This creates a half step, rather than a whole step, between the seventh and eighth notes of the scale, making the seventh a "leading tone."

D HARMONIC MINOR SCALE

MELODIC MINOR SCALES are created by raising the sixth and seventh notes of the natural minor scale while ascending, and returning them to natural minor (lowering them) while descending.

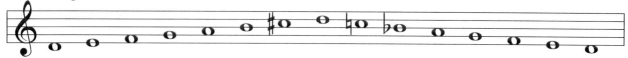

D MELODIC MINOR SCALE

The **CHROMATIC SCALE** is a series of thirteen notes. Each note is a half step away from its neighbor. Using sharps while the scale is ascending and flats while the scale is descending helps avoid the use of many naturals.

CHROMATIC SCALE BEGINNING ON F

The **WHOLE TONE SCALE** consists entirely of whole steps. There are only seven notes in the whole tone scale, so when writing the scale on the staff, one letter name will be missing.

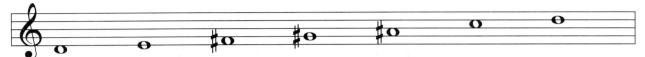

WHOLE TONE SCALE BEGINNING ON D

DORAN MODE contains the pattern of whole and half steps that occurs when beginning and ending on the SECOND note of the major scale. Half steps occur between notes 2-3 and 6-7.

DORIAN MODE ON D   **DORIAN MODE ON A**

PHRYGIAN MODE contains the pattern of whole and half steps that occurs when beginning and ending on theTHIRD note of the major scale. Half steps occur between notes 1-2 and 5-6.

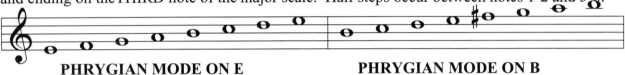

PHRYGIAN MODE ON E   **PHRYGIAN MODE ON B**

LYDIAN MODE contains the pattern of whole and half steps that occurs when beginning and ending on the FOURTH note of the major scale. Half steps occur between notes 4-5 and 7-8.

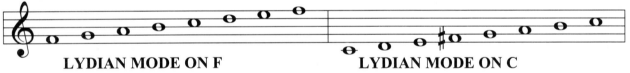

LYDIAN MODE ON F   **LYDIAN MODE ON C**

MIXOLYDIAN MODE contains the pattern of whole and half steps that occurs when beginning and ending on theFIFTH note of the major scale. Half steps occur between notes 3-4 and 6-7

MIXOLYDIAN MODE ON G   **MIXOLYDIAN MODE ON D**

AEOLIAN MODE contains the pattern of whole and half steps that occurs when beginning and ending on the SIXTH note of the major scale. It is the same as natural minor.

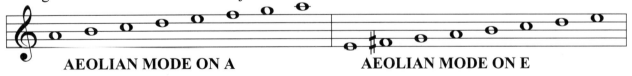

AEOLIAN MODE ON A   **AEOLIAN MODE ON E**

LOCRIAN MODE contains the pattern of whole and half steps that occurs when beginning and ending on theSEVENTH note of the major scale. Half steps occur between notes 1-2 and 4-5.

LOCRIAN MODE ON B   **LOCRIAN MODE ON F♯**

1. Write these scales.

Chromatic scale beginning on B (ascending and descending)

B Major

b natural minor

Whole Tone scale beginning on C♯

D♭ Major

g♯ harmonic minor

Mixolydian mode beginning on D

Locrian mode beginning on B

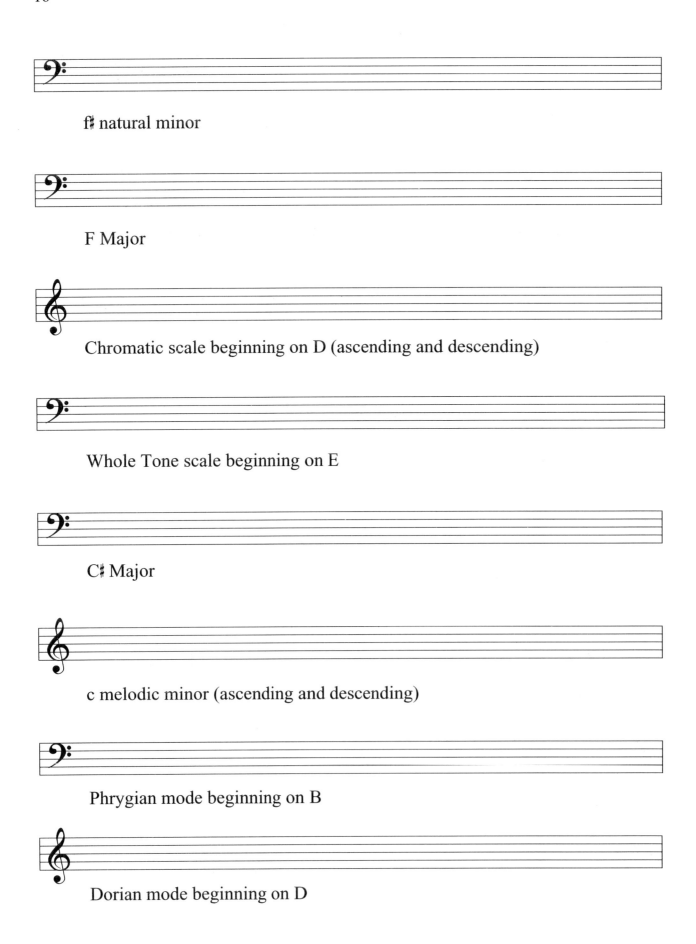

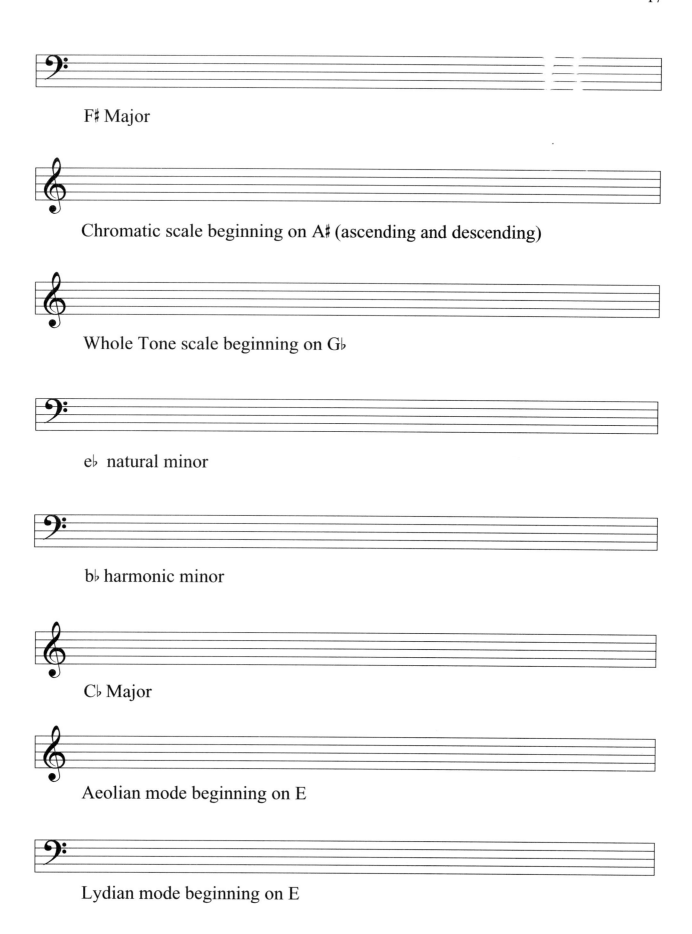

2. Give the name and type of scale circled in the examples below. For minor scales, be sure to tell which form of minor is used.

a. From *Invention No. 6* by J.S. Bach. _____ Scale

b. From *Song of War* by Schumann. _____ Scale

c. From *Sonata, op. 49, No. 1,* by Beethoven. _____ Scale

d. From *Bagatelle No. 2,* by Tcherepnin. _____ Scale

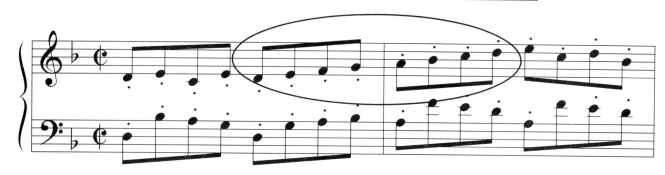

e. From *Sonatina, 1959*, by Khachaturian. _____ Scale

f. From *Little Fugue* by Schumann. _____ Scale

20

g. From *Sonata, Op. 49, No. 1,* by Beethoven. _____ Scale

h. From *Sonatina, 1959,* by Khachaturian. _____ Scale

i. From *Invention No. 8,* by J.S. Bach. _____ Scale

LESSON 3
INTERVALS

An **INTERVAL** is the distance between two notes. In music, intervals are named with numbers. When naming intervals, count the two notes that make the interval, and all the lines and spaces, or all the letter names, between the two.

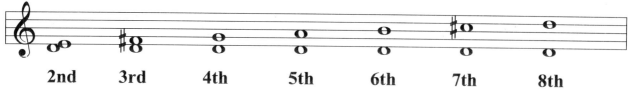

2nd   3rd   4th   5th   6th   7th   8th

HARMONIC INTERVALS occur when the two notes of the interval are played at the same time.

MELODIC INTERVALS occur when the two notes of the interval are played separately.

If the top note of the interval is within the key of the bottom note, the interval is **Major** or **Perfect**. 2nds, 3rds, 6ths, and 7ths are Major. 4ths, 5ths, and 8ths are perfect.

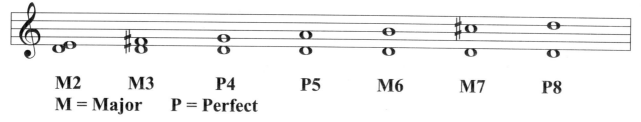

M2   M3   P4   P5   M6   M7   P8
M = Major   P = Perfect

If a Major 2nd, 3rd, 6th, or 7th is made smaller by lowering the top note or raising the bottom note a half step, without changing the letter name of either note, the interval becomes **minor**.

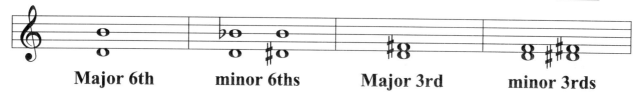

Major 6th   minor 6ths   Major 3rd   minor 3rds

If a Perfect 4th, 5th, or 8th is made smaller by lowering the top note or raising the bottom note a half step, without changing the letter name of either note, the interval becomes **diminished**.

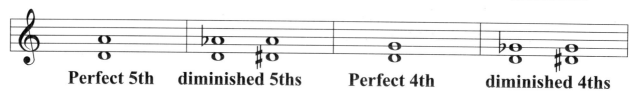

Perfect 5th   diminished 5ths   Perfect 4th   diminished 4ths

If a Major 2nd, 3rd, 6th, or 7th is made smaller by lowering the top note or raising the bottom note a whole step, without changing the letter name of either note, the interval becomes **diminished**.

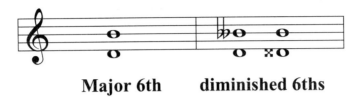

Major 6th   diminished 6ths

If a Major or Perfect interval is made larger by raising the top note or lowering the bottom note a half step, without changing the letter name of either note, the interval becomes **Augmented.**

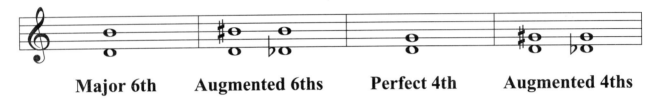

Major 6th   Augmented 6ths   Perfect 4th   Augmented 4ths

To write an interval above a given note, determine the key signature for the lower note, and add any necessary accidentals. For Major or Perfect intervals, keep those accidentals. For minor, diminished, or Augmented intervals, raise or lower the top note without changing the letter name.

In the example below, an Augmented 4th above F is needed. F Major has B♭. The 4th is made Augmented by removing the B♭ (raising the note a half step).

A4 up   Answer: B

To write an interval below a given note, determine all possibilities the note could be. Then, determine which of those notes is the correct one for the quality of the interval needed.

In the example below, a minor 7th below C is needed. The three possibilities are D, D♭, and D♯. A minor 7th above D♭ is C♭, a minor 7th above D♯ is C♯, and a minor 7th above D is C. The answer is D.

m7 below C   Answer: D

1. Name these intervals. Give their qualities (Major, minor, Perfect, Augmented, or diminished), and number names (2nd, 3rd, etc.). The first one is given.

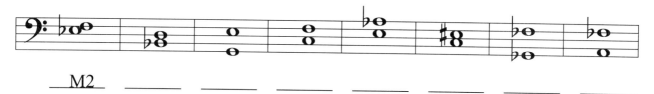

   M2   _____   _____   _____   _____   _____   _____   _____

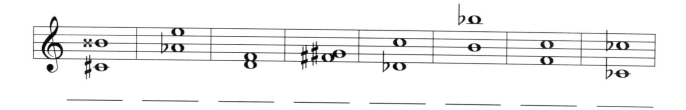

   _____   _____   _____   _____   _____   _____   _____   _____

2. Complete these intervals. Do note change the given note.

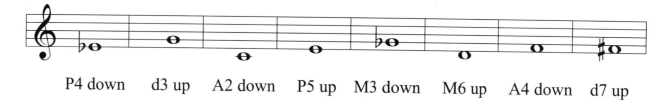

   P4 down   d3 up   A2 down   P5 up   M3 down   M6 up   A4 down   d7 up

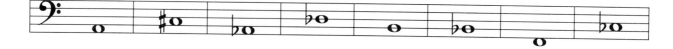

   d2 down   P8 up   d5 up   m6 down   A8 down   m7 up   A6 up   M2 down

24

When naming intervals within music literature, follow these steps:

a. Write the sharps or flats from the key signature, or from earlier in the measure, before the notes (as reminders).

b. Determine the number for the interval (by counting the lines and spaces, or the letter names).

c. Using the key signature for the <u>lowest note of the interval</u>, find the quality (Major, minor, Perfect, diminished, or Augmented).

3. Name the circled intervals in the passages below. Follow the steps listed above for each interval.

   a. From *La fille aux cheveux de lin* by Debussy.

   _____

   b. From *Waltz, Op. Posth. 69, No. 1,* by Chopin.

   _____

   c. From *Sonata, Op. 49, No. 1,* by Beethoven.

   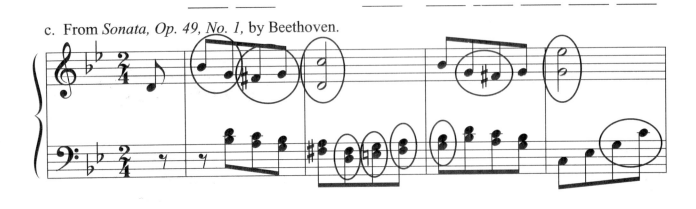

   _____

LESSON 4
DIATONIC AND CHROMATIC HALF STEPS*

A piece of music is considered **DIATONIC** when it is based on a particular Major or minor scale.

The term **DIATONIC HALF STEP** comes from the natural occurance of half steps in the Major scale. For example, in D Major Scale, diatonic half steps occur between F# and G, and between C# and D. In minor keys, half steps which include the harmonic or melodic minor notes are also diatonic. Some theory scholars use this as the definition for diatonic half step.

Another use of the term **DIATONIC HALF STEP** is to mean any half step which uses two different letter names, such as C# to D, or E to F. This is the definition used in this workbook. The diatonic half steps are circled in this example, from *Gathering of the Grapes--Happy Time!*, by Schumann.

CHROMATIC HALF STEPS are defined by some as half steps which do not occur naturally within the scale. For example, in a D Major scale, D to E♭ would be a chromatic half step, since it is not contained within the scale. A second definition is any half step that is written using the same letter name, such as C-C# or E♭ to E. This is the definition used in this workbook.

The chromatic half steps are circled in the example below, from *Gathering of the Grapes--Happy Time!*, by Schumann.

*Scholarly theory texts are divided concerning the definition of diatonic and chromatic half steps.

1. Write diatonic half steps above these notes.

2. Write chromatic half steps above these notes.

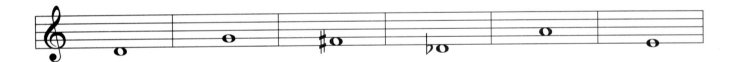

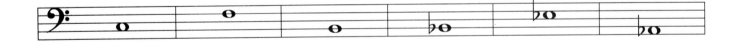

3. Several half steps are circled in the examples below. Tell whether each is a diatonic or chromatic half step.

   a. From *Sonatina* by Khachaturian. Key of: _____

_____ _____ _____

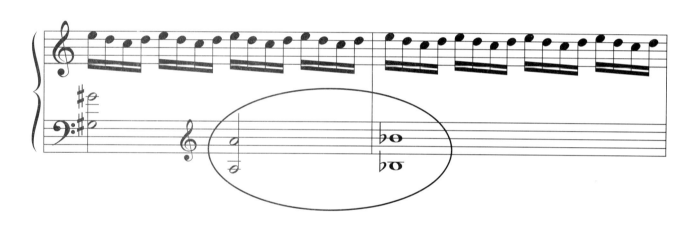

_____

   b. From *Sonatina* by Khachaturian. Key of: _____

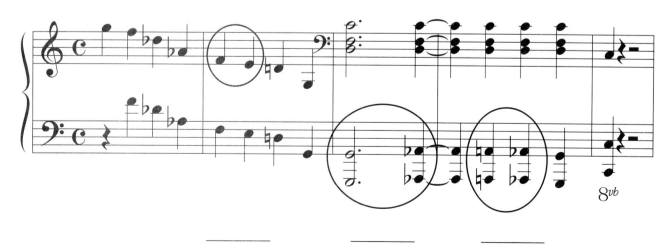

_____ _____ _____

c. From *Sonata, Op. 49, No. 1,* by Beethoven. Key of: _____

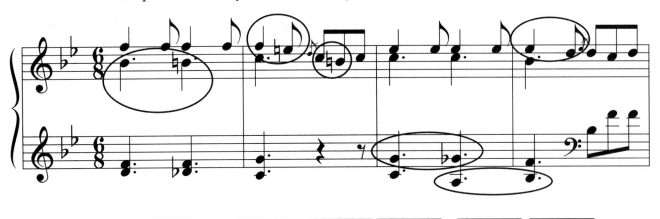

d. From *Nocturne in c♯ minor* by Chopin. Key of: _____

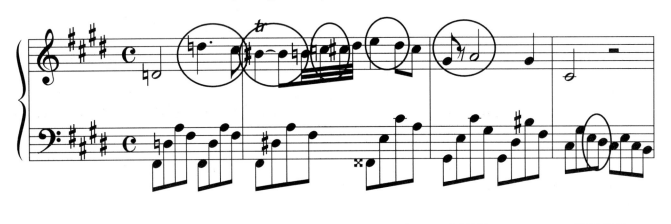

LESSON 5
MAJOR, MINOR, AUGMENTED AND DIMINISHED TRIADS AND INVERSIONS

A <u>**TRIAD**</u> is a chord which contains three notes.

D Major Triad

<u>**MAJOR TRIADS**</u> are made up of the first, third, and fifth notes of the Major scale with the same letter name. The lowest note of a Major triad in root position (see example) names the triad.

D Major Scale   D Major Root Position Triad

To change a Major triad into a <u>**MINOR**</u> triad, lower the middle note (the third) a half step. Minor triads have the same sharps or flats found in the minor key signature with the same letter name.

D Major Triad   d minor triad

To change a Major triad into an <u>**AUGMENTED**</u> triad, raise the top note (the fifth) a half step. The intervals between the notes are both Major 3rds.

D Major Triad   D Augmented Triad

To change a Major triad into a **DIMINISHED** triad, lower the middle note (the third) <u>and</u> the top note (the fifth) a half step each. The intervals between the notes are both minor 3rds.

D Major Triad   **d diminished triad**

1. Write these triads.

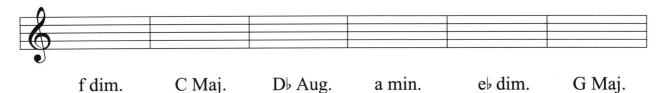

    f dim.   C Maj.   D♭ Aug.   a min.   e♭ dim.   G Maj.

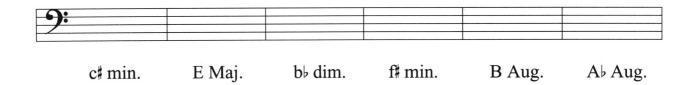

    c♯ min.   E Maj.   b♭ dim.   f♯ min.   B Aug.   A♭ Aug.

2. Name these triads with their roots (letter names) and qualities (Major, minor, Augmented, or diminished). (The first one is given.)

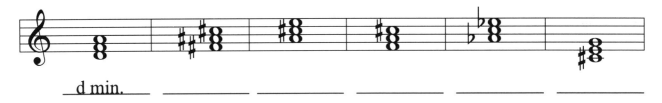

  d min.   _____   _____   _____   _____   _____

  _____   _____   _____   _____   _____   _____

A **ROOT POSITION TRIAD** occurs when the note which names the triad is on the bottom. Root position triads are called $\frac{5}{3}$ triads, because when the triad is in its simplest position, the intervals from the bottom note are a 5th and a 3rd. When labelling a triad in root position, only the letter name and quality are needed.

D Major Root Position Triad

D Major or D Major $\frac{5}{3}$

A **FIRST INVERSION TRIAD** occurs when the **third** or **middle** note of the triad is the lowest note. First inversion triads are called $\frac{6}{3}$ triads, because when they are in their simplest position (with the notes close together) they contain the intervals of a 6th and a 3rd above the bottom note.

When labelling first inversion triads, the symbol 6 (or $\frac{6}{3}$) is used beside the name of the triad.

D Major Root Position Triad   **D Major First Inversion Triad**

D Major or D Major $\frac{5}{3}$ **D Major ^{6} or D Major $\frac{6}{3}$**

A **SECOND INVERSION TRIAD** occurs when the **fifth** or **top** note of the triad is on the bottom. Second inversion triads are called $\frac{6}{4}$ triads, because when they are in their simplest position (with the notes close together) they contain the intervals of a 6th and a 4th above the bottom note.

When labelling second inversion triads, the symbol $\frac{6}{4}$ is used beside the name of the triad.

D Major   **D Major**   **D Major**
Root Position   **First Inversion**   **Second**
Triad   **Triad**   **Inversion**
D Major   **D Major ^{6}**   **Triad**
or D Major $\frac{5}{3}$ **or D Major $\frac{6}{3}$**   **D Major $\frac{6}{4}$**

3. Write these triads in root position, first inversion, and second inversion. (The first one given.)

d diminished   C♯ Major

E Augmented   E♭ Major

a♭ minor   G Augmented

c diminished   f minor

B Major   A Augmented

f♯ diminished   b♭ minor

4. Name these triads with their roots, qualities, and inversions (figured bass). (The first one is given.)

 eb minor⁶
(or eb minor ⁶₃)

5. Write these triads.

C Maj.⁶   d min.⁶   Ab Aug. ⁶₄   db dim.   a min. ⁶₄   D Aug.⁶

Eb Maj. ⁶₄   f min.⁶   B Maj. ⁶₄   cb dim.   f# dim.   e min. ⁶₄

E Maj.   G Aug.   c# min.⁶   gb dim. ⁶₄   Bb Aug.⁶   a dim.⁶

In actual music, triads are rarely in their simplest positions. To determine the letter name and quality of a triad within a piece, follow these steps:

a. Put the triad in its simplest form by placing the letter names so that there is one letter between each (for example, F-C-F-A becomes F-A-C).

b. Add all sharps or flats from the key signature, or from earlier in the measure, to the letter names.

c. Determine the letter name and quality of the triad.

d. Determine the inversion of the triad by looking at the lowest note on the <u>lowest</u> staff.

Example (From *Minuet in G* by Beethoven):

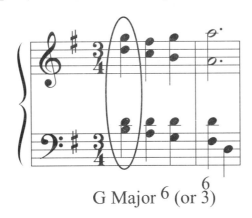

G Major ^{6} (or $^6_3$)

a. Notes are B-D-D-G.

b. Simplest form is G-B-D.

c. G Major Triad.

d. B is the lowest note (in the bass clef), so the triad is in first inversion ($^6_3$).

e. G Major ^{6} (or G Major $^6_3$)

If only two notes are present in a literature example, and when they are simplified they create the interval of a third, they will most likely be the root and third of the chord. If one note occurs twice, it is most likely the root. (See example 1.)

If the two notes create the interval of a fifth when simplified, they will be the root and fifth. (See example 2.)

It is very rare that the two notes will represent the third and fifth of the chord. (See example 3.)

Ex. 1. G Major Triad Root and Third	2. G Major Triad Root and Fifth	3. G Major Triad Third and Fifth
Common	Occasional	Rare

6. Name the circled triads in the examples below by giving their roots, qualitites, and inversions (figured bass).

a. From *La fille aux cheveux de lin* by Debussy.

b. From *Sonata, op. 49, No. 1,* by Beethoven.

c. From *Kinderscenen, Op. 15, No. 6,* by Schumann.

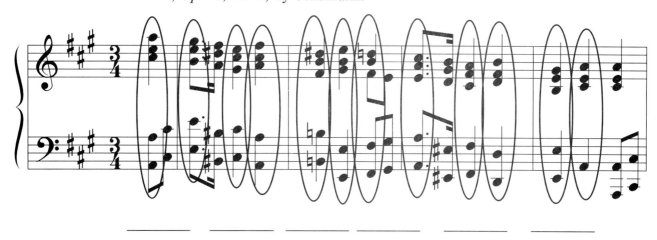

d. From *Song of War* by Schumann.

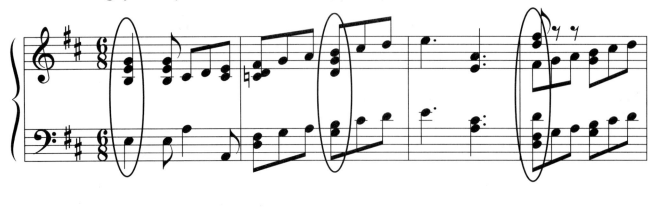

e. From *Sonatina (1959)* by Khachaturian.

f. From *Little Fugue* by Schumann.

LESSON 6
PRIMARY AND SECONDARY TRIADS
FIGURED BASS

A triad can be built on each note of the scale.

When building triads on scale tones, all of the sharps or flats that are in the key being used must be added to the chords which have those notes.

Example: D Major Scale has F♯ and C♯. When writing the triads of D Major, every time an F or C appears in a chord, a sharp must be added to it. (See example below.)

Triads of the scale are numbered using Roman Numerals. Upper case Roman Numerals are used for Major triads, lower case Roman Numerals are used for minor triads, upper case Roman Numerals with "+" are used for Augmented triads, and lower case Roman Numerals with "o" are used for diminished triads. These are called the **FIGURED BASS SYMBOLS.**

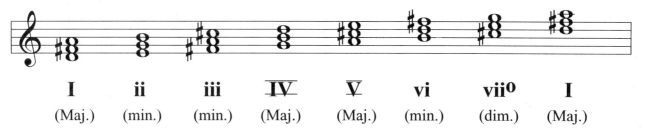

PRIMARY AND SECONDARY TRIADS IN THE KEY OF D MAJOR

I, IV, and V are the **PRIMARY TRIADS**. In Major keys, these three triads are Major, and are the most commonly used chords for harmonizing tonal melodies. The chords are labelled with upper case Roman Numerals.

ii, iii, vi, and vii⁰ are the **SECONDARY TRIADS**. In Major keys, ii, iii, and vi are minor, and vii⁰ is diminished. The chords are labelled with lower case Roman Numerals, and the vii⁰ chord has a small circle beside the Roman Numeral.

The qualities of the triads in minor keys are different from those for Major keys. When using **harmonic minor**, the triads have the following qualities:

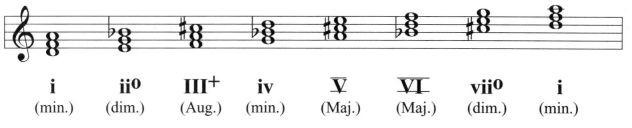

PRIMARY AND SECONDARY TRIADS IN THE KEY OF D MINOR

1. Write the Primary and Secondary Triads for these keys, and label the triads with Roman Numerals. Circle each Primary Triad, and put a box around each Secondary Triad. Do not use a key signature. Write the sharps or flats before the notes. (The first one is given.)

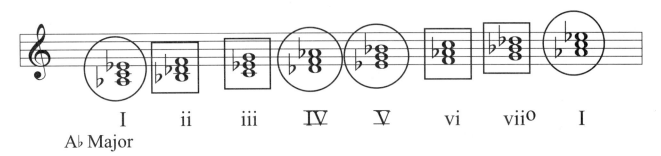

      I   ii   iii   IV   V   vi   vii°   I

A♭ Major

g minor

F♯ Major

b minor

D♭ Major

c♯ minor

2. Write the Primary Triads for these keys, and label the triads with Roman Numerals. Do not use a key signature. Write the sharps or flats before the notes. (The first one is given.)

3. Write the Secondary Triads for these keys, and label the triads with Roman Numerals. Do not use a key signature. Write the sharps or flats before the notes. (The first one is given.)

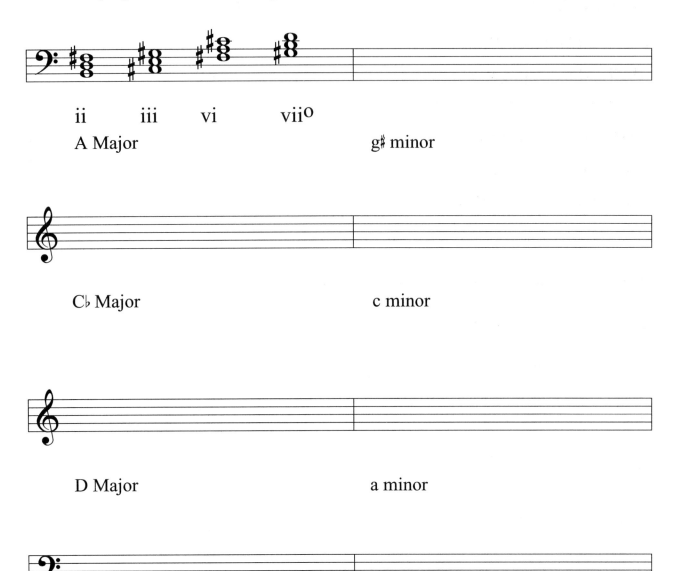

Each degree of the scale has a name. These are called the **SCALE DEGREE NAMES:**

The **I** chord is **TONIC**.

The **ii** chord is **SUPERTONIC**.

The **iii** chord is **MEDIANT**.

The **IV** chord is **SUBDOMINANT**.

The **V** chord is **DOMINANT**.

The **vi** chord is **SUBMEDIANT**.

The **vii°** chord is **LEADING TONE**.

(Note: Qualities used above are from Major keys. The names stay the same when in minor.)

4. Match these Roman Numerals with their scale degree names.

    a. ii   _____ Submediant

    b. I   _____ Dominant

    c. iii   _____ Supertonic

    d. vii°   _____ Subdominant

    e. IV   _____ Leading Tone

    f. vi   _____ Mediant

    g. V   _____ Tonic

5. Write the scale degree names for these Roman Numerals.

    I   _____

    ii   _____

    iii   _____

    IV   _____

    V   _____

    vi   _____

    vii°   _____

In actual music, chords are rarely in their simplest position. To determine the Roman Numeral of a chord within a piece, do the following:

a. Determine the Major or minor key of the piece.

b. Put the chord in its simplest form by placing the letter names so that there is one letter between each (for example, F-C-F-A becomes F-A-C).

c. Add all sharps or flats from the key signature or from earlier in the measure to the letter names.

d. Determine the Roman Numeral of the chord by counting from the letter name of the key up to the name of the chord.

e. Determine the inversion of the chord by looking at the lowest note (on the <u>lowest</u> staff).

Example (From *Minuet in G* by Beethoven):

a. Key of G Major

b. Notes are: F#-D-A-A

c. Simplest form is: D-F#-A

d. D Major Triad. The piece is in the key of G Major. D is the fifth note of the G Major Scale; therefore, this is the V chord.

e. The lowest note (in the bass clef) is F#. The chord is in first inversion. Label the chord V$^6_3$, (or V^6).

6. Label the circled chords below. Put the Roman Numeral and figured bass (inversion) for each.

   a. From *A Little Canon* by Schumann. Key of: _____

   _____   _____ _____ _____   _____   _____

   b. From *Nocturne, Brown-Index 49,* by Chopin. Key of: _____

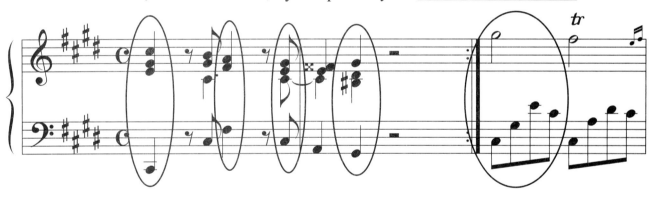

   _____   _____ _____ _____

   _____

c. From *Waltz, Op. 34, No. 2,* by Chopin. Key of: _____

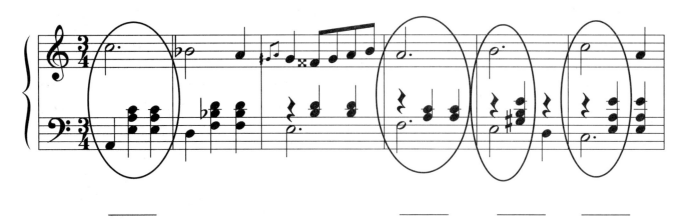

d. From *Waltz, Op. 3, No. 2,* by Britten. Key of: _____

e. From *Kinderscenen, Op. 15, No. 1,* by Schumann. Key of: _____

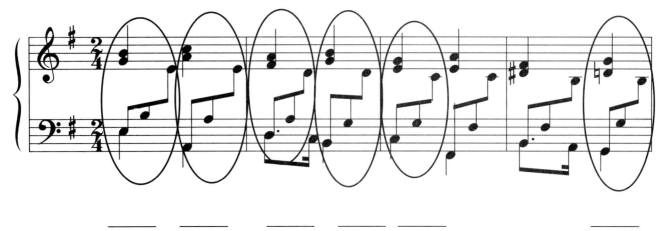

LESSON 7
DOMINANT AND DIMINISHED SEVENTH CHORDS

The **DOMINANT SEVENTH CHORD** is created when a fourth note is added to the V chord (the Dominant chord). This fourth note is a seventh above the root of the chord, giving it the name "Dominant 7th." The chord consists of a Major triad on the bottom, with the added interval of a minor 7th.

The Dominant Seventh is so named because it is based on the V or Dominant chord, and has the interval of a 7th within the chord.

To write Dominant Seventh chords within a given key, go to the fifth note of the key, and write a V chord. Then, add the note which is a minor 7th above the root of the chord. When in harmonic minor, the third of the chord (which is the leading tone or 7th note of the key) must be raised a half-step.

These are the Inversions of the Dominant Seventh (abbreviated and full figured bass is shown):

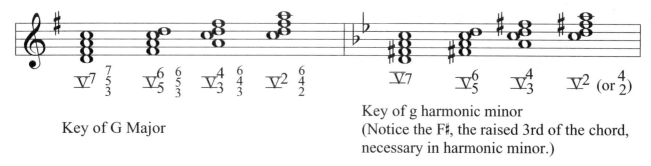

Key of G Major

Key of g harmonic minor
(Notice the F♯, the raised 3rd of the chord, necessary in harmonic minor.)

Dominant Seventh chords can be on a given note, or in a given key. When asked to write a Dominant Seventh on a given note, write a Major triad with an added minor seventh.

When asked to write a Dominant Seventh in a given key, find the V chord for that key, and add a note which is a minor seventh above the root. In Major keys, no accidentals will be added to the chord. In minor keys, the third will be raised because of harmonic minor.

Dominant 7th on D   **Dominant 7th in the key of D Major**

1. Write Dominant Seventh chords and their inversions in the following keys, and label the chords with Roman Numerals and figured bass. Be sure to use harmonic minor. The first one is given.

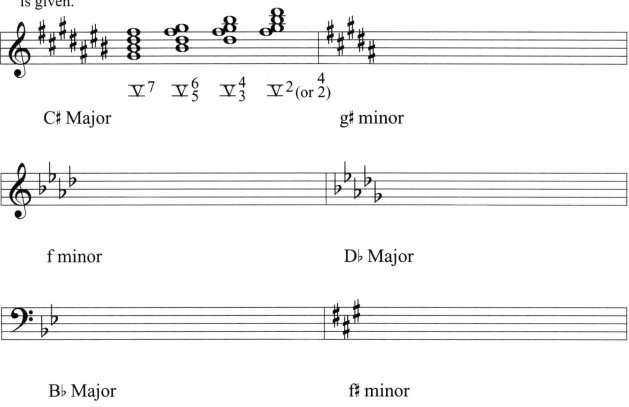

C♯ Major

g♯ minor

f minor

D♭ Major

B♭ Major

f♯ minor

2. Write Dominant 7th chords and their inversions on these notes.

The **DIMINISHED SEVENTH CHORD** consists of a diminished triad, with the interval of a diminished seventh added to the top.

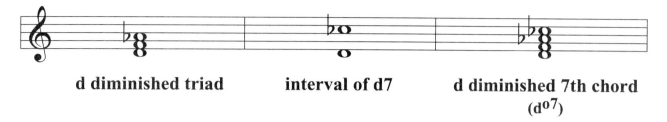

Inversions of the diminished 7th chord are as follows:

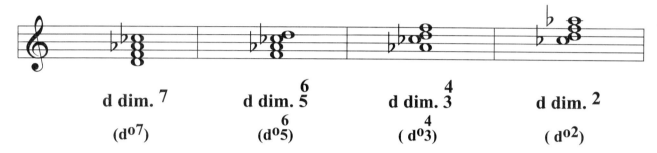

3. Write these diminished 7th chords and their inversions. (The first one is given.)

4. Label the circled seventh chord in each example below. Some are Dominant 7th chords, and some are diminished 7th chords. Label the Dominant 7th chords with their Roman Numerals and figured bass ($V7$, V^6_5, etc.). Label the diminished 7th chords with their letter names and inversions (c dim. 7 or c^{o7}).

a. From *Mazurka, Op. 67, No. 4,* by Chopin.

b. From *Sonata Op. 49, No. 1,* by Beethoven.

c. From *Kinderscenen, Op. 15, No. 6,* by Schumann.

d. From *Song of War* by Schumann.

e. From *Sonata, Op. 49, No. 1,* by Beethoven.

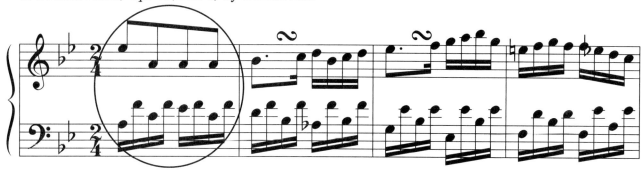

f. From *Sonatina, 1959,* by Khachaturian.

g. From *Little Fugue* by Schumann.

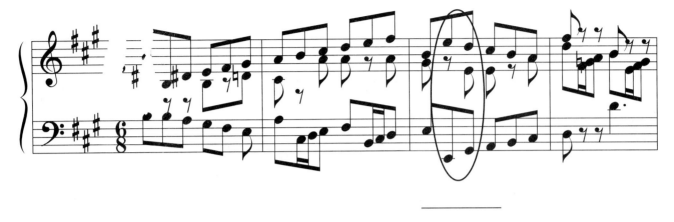

h. From *Sonata, Op. 49, No. 1,* by Beethoven.

i. From *Nocturne in c♯ minor* by Chopin.

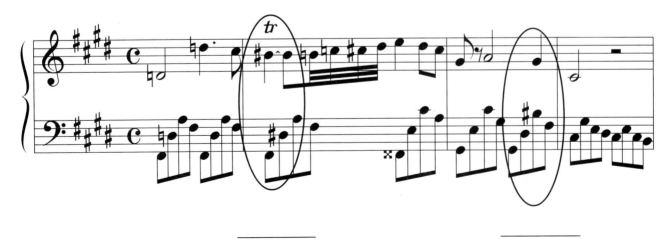

LESSON 8
THE SECONDARY DOMINANT

Many times, a composer will use chords which are not within the key of the piece of music. One of the most common of these is the **SECONDARY DOMINANT**.

The Secondary Dominant is so named because it is the Dominant (V) of a key other than Tonic (I). It is usually followed by the chord which would be a I chord of the key to which it belongs. The qualities of secondary dominants are different from those of the regular primary and secondary triads.

Examples in the key of C Major:

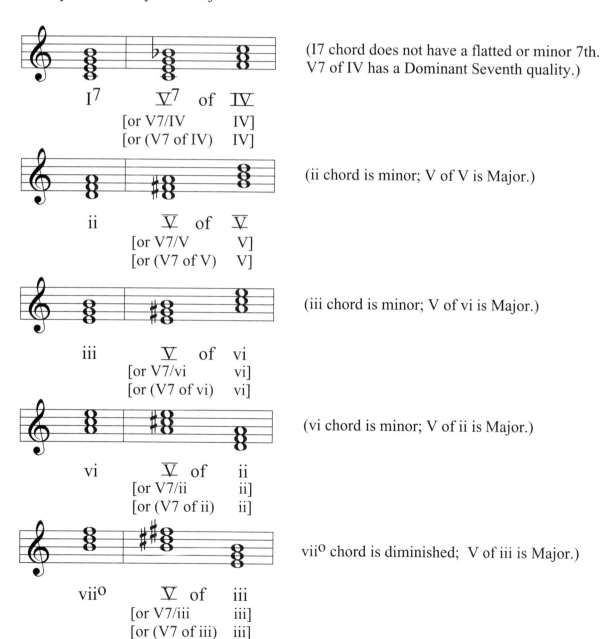

(I7 chord does not have a flatted or minor 7th. V7 of IV has a Dominant Seventh quality.)

(ii chord is minor; V of V is Major.)

(iii chord is minor; V of vi is Major.)

(vi chord is minor; V of ii is Major.)

vii° chord is diminished; V of iii is Major.)

51

1. Write these Secondary Dominants. Determine whether to use the Major or minor key by the quality of the second Roman Numeral. V of V examples have "Major" or "minor" written beside them. Remember to use harmonic minor. Follow the steps in the example below to write each one.

a. Find the chord which represents the <u>second</u> Roman Numeral (for example, for V of IV, find the IV chord of the given key).

b. Find the V (or V7) chord for that second chord. (For example, if the IV chord is C Major, count up five notes to G Major chord.

c. Write the Secondary Dominant chord, followed by the chord represented by the second Roman Numeral.

Example: V$_5^6$ of iii in the key of A Major.

a. Find the iii chord in A Major: c# minor chord.

b. Find the V7 chord of c# minor: G#7.

c. Write G#$_5^6$ (the inversion of G#7) followed by c# minor (the iii chord).

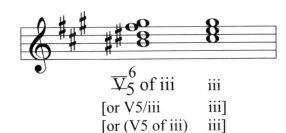

V$_5^6$ of iii   iii
[or V5/iii   iii]
[or (V5 of iii)   iii]

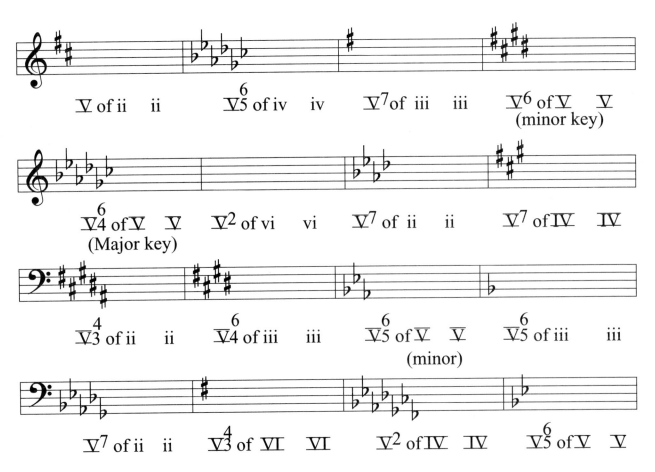

When labelling Secondary Dominants in music literature, follow these steps:

a. Determine the Major or minor key of the piece.

b. Label the Secondary Dominant (the first of the two chords) using, for example, "V of IV." Be sure to include the figured bass for the V chord.

c. Label the second chord with its Roman Numeral and figured bass symbol.

d. The two chords will be labelled, for example, "V of iii   iii" or "V/iii   iii."

Example: From *A Little Canon* by Schumann.

a. Key of A Major.

b. The first chord's letter name is A Dominant 7th. This is the dominant of D, which is the IV chord. Label the chord V7 of IV.

c. The second chord, the IV chord, is in second inversion. Label the chord IV$_4^6$.

d. Chords are labelled V^7 of IV   IV$_4^6$ or V^7/IV   IV$_4^6$.

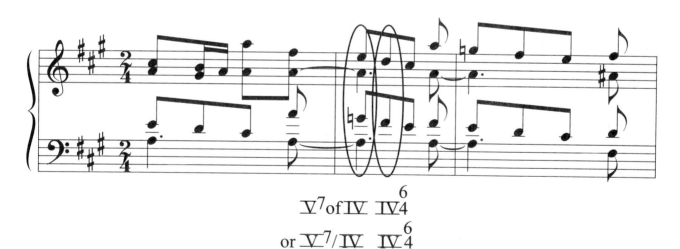

V^{7}of IV   IV$_4^6$
or V^7/IV   IV$_4^6$

2. Label the Secondary Dominants in these excerpts with "V of ___," then label the following chord with its Roman Numeral. (Be sure to add the figured bass symbols, that is, the inversion numbers, to all chords. The first one is given.)

a. From *A Little Canon* by Schumann. Key of: _____ Major

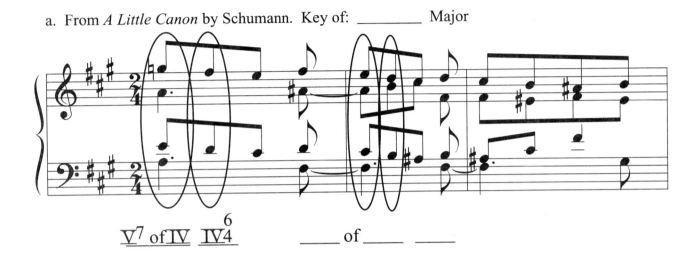

V⁷ of IV   IV⁶₄   ___ of ___   ___

b. From *Nocturne, Brown-Index 49,* by Chopin. Key of: _____ minor

___ of ___   ___

c. From *Waltz, Op. 34, No. 2,* by Chopin. Key of: _____ minor

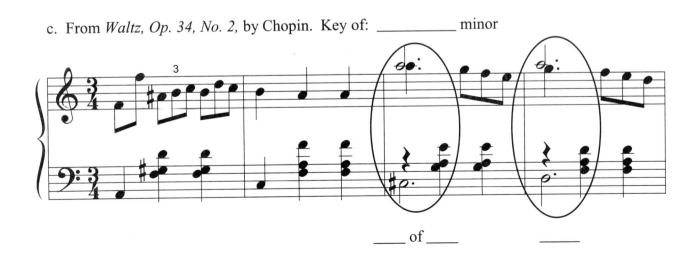

___ of ___   ___

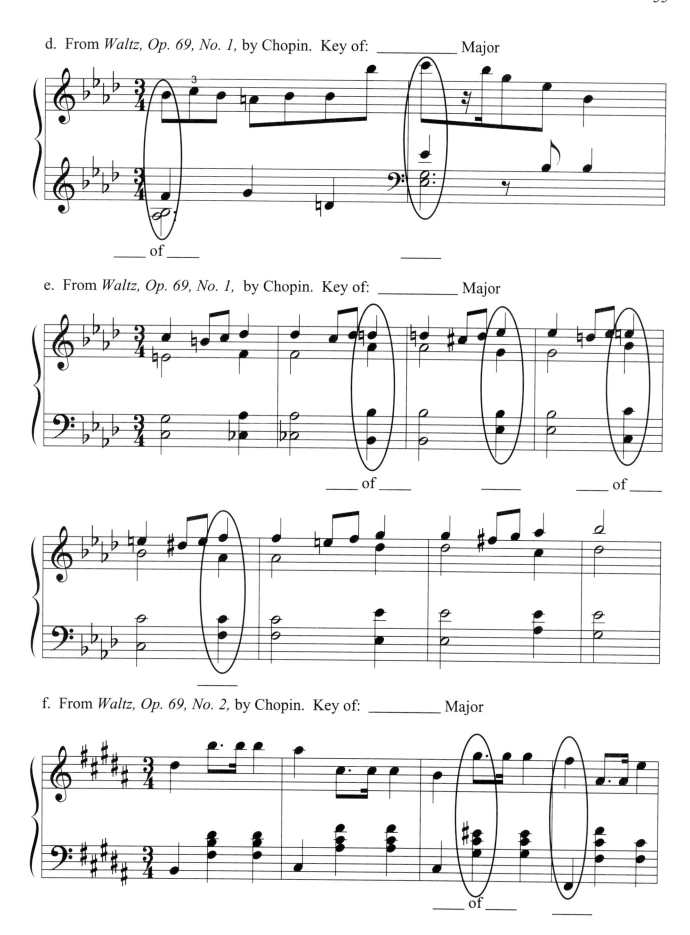

g. From *French Suite No. VI: Gavotte* by J.S. Bach. Key of: _____ Major

h. From *Bunte Blatter, Op. 99, No. 3,* by Schumann. Key of _____ Major

i. From *Bunte Blatter, Op. 99, No. 3,* by Schumann. Key of: _____ Major

j. From *Bunte Blatter, Op. 99, No. 3,* by Schumann. Key of: _____ Major

LESSON 9
AUTHENTIC, HALF, PLAGAL, AND DECEPTIVE CADENCES; CHORD PROGRESSIONS

A **CADENCE** is a closing or ending for a musical phrase, made up of a combination of chords. There are many types of cadences. Four common cadences are:

AUTHENTIC, HALF, PLAGAL, and DECEPTIVE CADENCES

An **AUTHENTIC CADENCE** consists of a V or V^7 chord followed by a I chord:

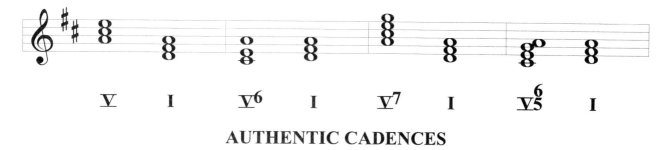

AUTHENTIC CADENCES

1. Write Authentic Cadences in these keys, using the chords indicated by the Roman Numerals. Determine whether to use the Major or minor key by the quality of the Roman Numerals. (The first one is given.)

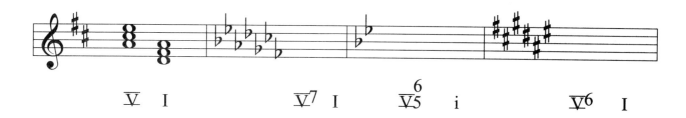

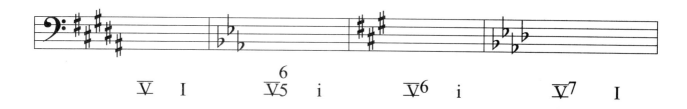

A **PLAGAL CADENCE** consists of a IV chord followed by a I chord:

PLAGAL CADENCES

2. Write Plagal Cadences in these keys, using the chords indicated by the Roman Numerals. (The first one is given.)

A **HALF CADENCE** is a cadence which ends with a V or V^7 chord:

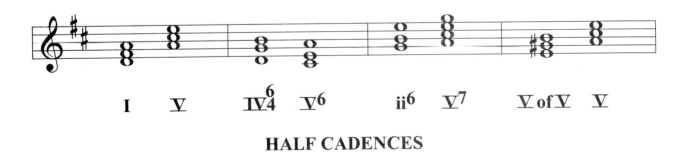

HALF CADENCES

3. Write Half Cadences in these keys, using the chords indicated by the Roman Numerals. (The first one is given.) Be sure to use harmonic minor.

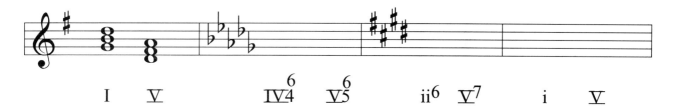

I   V   IV$^6_4$ V$^6_5$ ii^6 V^7 i   V

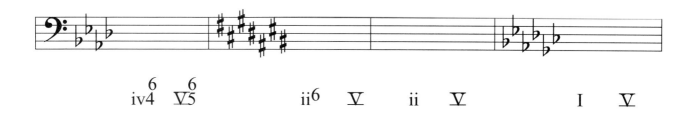

iv$^6_4$ V$^6_5$ ii^6 V   ii   V   I   V

A **DECEPTIVE CADENCE** consists of a V (or sometimes IV) chord followed by a vi chord:

V   vi   IV   vi

DECEPTIVE CADENCES

4. Write Deceptive Cadences in these keys, using the chords indicated by the Roman Numerals. (The first one is given.)

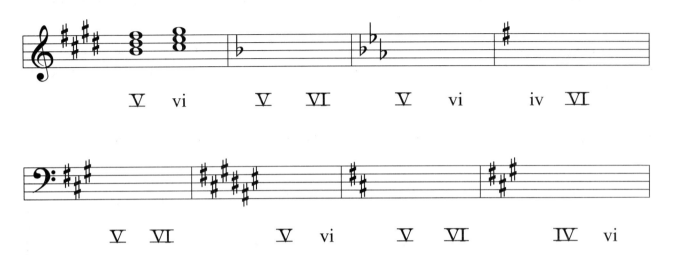

5. Label the chords of each of these cadences with Roman Numerals and inversion numbers, then put the type of cadence (Authentic, Half, Plagal, or Deceptive) on the line below the Roman Numerals. (The first one is given.)

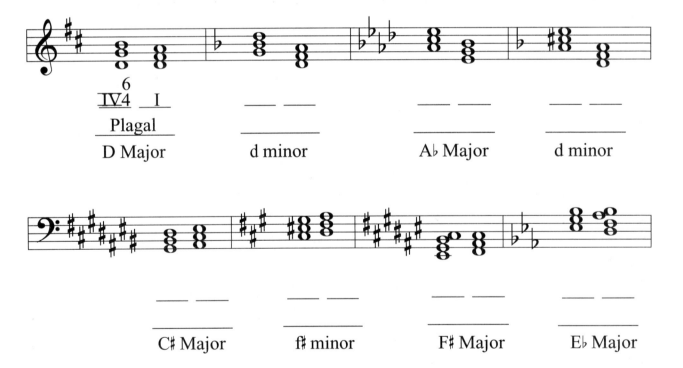

A **CHORD PROGRESSION** is created by combining certain chords from a given key, using various positions for the chords to make a smooth progression. Each of the following chord progressions **MODULATES** to a new key. A secondary dominant is used to transition into the new key. (See more on modulation in Lesson 12.)

The **PIVOT CHORD** is a chord that precedes a chord change, and is common to both the original key and the key to which the music modulates. The pivot chord is circled in each example.

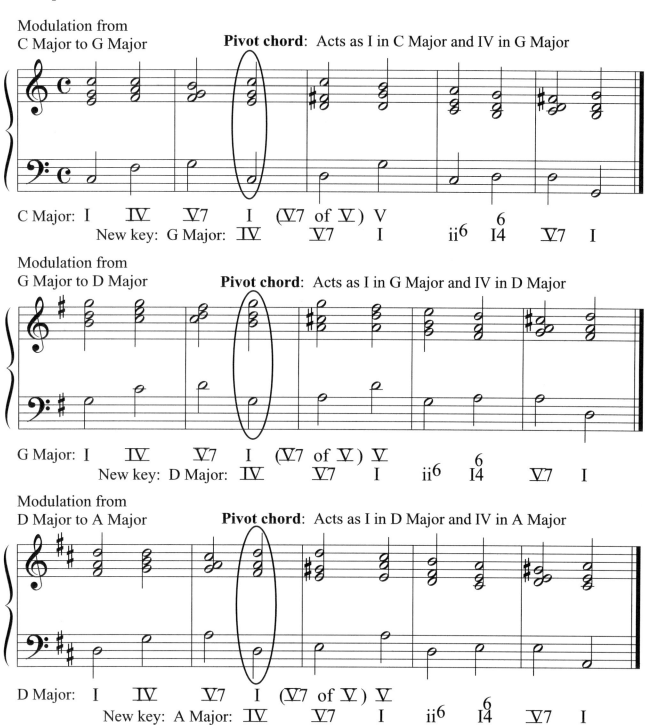

6. a. Label the chords used in these chord progressions with Roman numerals and figured bass. Circle each pivot chord.

b. Write these chord progressions. Circle each pivot chord.

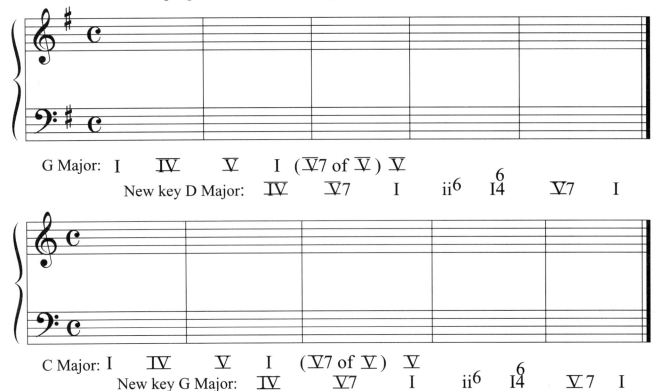

When labelling cadences in music literature, label the last two chords of a phrase with their Roman Numerals. These are the two chords which make up the cadence. Then, give the cadence its name (Authentic, Half, Plagal, or Deceptive).

Example (From *Waltz, Op. posth. 69, No. 1,* by Chopin.): Key of A♭ Major, Authentic Cadence

7. Name the cadence at the end of each phrase below. Give the name of the Major or minor key, write the Roman Numerals for the last two chords, and name the type of cadence (Authentic, Half, Plagal, or Deceptive).

a. From *La fille aux cheveux de lin* by Debussy.

Key of: _____

Type of Cadence: _____

b. From *Kinderscenen, Op. 15, no. 6,* by Schumann.

Key of: _____

Type of Cadence: _____

c. From *Nocturne, Brown-Index 49,* by Chopin.

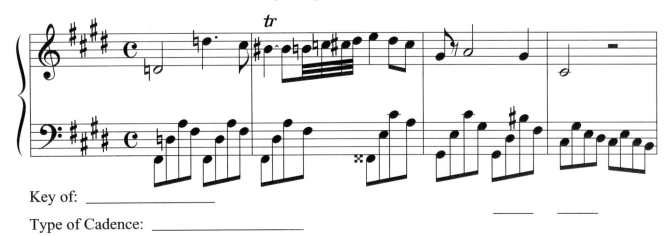

Key of: _____

Type of Cadence: _____

d. From *A Little Canon* by Schumann.

Key of: _____

Type of Cadence: _____

e. From *Waltz, Op. 34, No. 2*, by Chopin.

Key of: _____

Type of Cadence: _____

f. From *Waltz, Op. 69, No. 1,* by Chopin.

Key of: _____   ____ ____

Type of Cadence: _____

g. From *Bunte Blatter, Op. 99, No. 3,* by Schumann.

Key of: _____   ____ ____

Type of Cadence: _____

h. From *Waltz, Op. 34, No. 2,* by Chopin.

Key of: _____   ____   ____

Type of Cadence: _____

i. From *A Little Canon* by Schumann.

Key of: _____

Type of Cadence: _____

j. From *Song of War* by Schumann.

Key of: _____

Type of Cadence: _____

k. From *Figured Chorale* by Schumann.

Key of: _____

Type of Cadence: _____

LESSON 10
MODULATION

MODULATION occurs when a musical composition changes from the original key to another key, and remains in the new key for a reasonable amount of time.

A piece of music may modulate to any key, but frequently either the Dominant (V) key or the relative Major or minor is used.

In the example below, from *Song of War* by Schumann, the music begins in the key of D Major, and modulates to the key of F♯ Major.

Two important 20th Century theorists, Schoenberg and Schenker, taught that music does not truly modulate, but that sections of music which appear to modulate are essentially extended cadences, and that these sections are not much different in essence from sections which use any chord other than tonic.

1. In the following excerpts, give the name of the original key, and the name of the key to which the music modulates.

a. From *Gathering of the Grapes--Happy Time!* by Schumann.

Original key: _____ Modulates to: _____

b. From *Waltz, Op. posth. 69, No. 1,* by Chopin.

Original key: _____ Modulates to: _____

c. From *Waltz, Op. 69, No. 2,* by Chopin.

Original key: _____ Modulates to: _____

d. From *Nocturne, Brown-Index 49,* by Chopin.

Original key: _____ Modulates to: _____

This page has purposely been left blank.

REVIEW
TERMS USED IN LESSONS 1-10

Authentic Cadence: A V-I cadence (in harmomic minor, V-i).

Cadence: A closing or ending for a phrase of music, made up of two or more chords.

Chromatic Half Step: A half step which does not occur naturally within the key of the music.

Chromatic Scale: A scale made up entirely of half steps.

Deceptive Cadence: a V-vi cadence (in harmonic minor, V-VI).

Diatonic Half Step: A half step which occurs naturally within the key of the music.

Diminished Seventh Chord: A four note chord made up of a diminished triad, and a diminished 7th above the root.

Dominant Seventh: A four note chord made up of a Major triad, and a minor 7th above the root. Root position is V^7, first inversion is V 6/5, second inversion is V 4/3, and third inversion is V^2.

Figured Bass: Symbols used to denote the inversion of a chord (such as 6, 6/4, 6/5, 4/3, or 2).

First Inversion: A triad written with the third as the lowest note. The figured bass symbol for a triad in first inversion is 6/3, or 6. The figured bass symbol for a seventh chord in first in 6/5/3, or 6/5.

Half Cadence: A cadence which ends with the V chord.

Interval: The distance between two notes, named with numbers. Intervals may be Major, Perfect, minor, diminished, or Augmented.

Inversion: A triad written in a position in which the note that names the triad is not the lowest.

Key Signature: The sharps or flats at the beginning of a piece of music. (There are Major and minor key signatures.)

Modulation: A key change within a composition.

Plagal Cadence: A IV-I cadence (in harmonic minor, iv-i).

Primary Triads: The I, IV, and V chords. (In minor, i, iv, and V.)

Root Position: A traid written in a position so that the note which names it is the lowest. The figured bass symbol for a triad in root position is 5/3. The figured bass symbol for a seventh chord in root position is 7/5/3, or 7.

Scale: A series of notes in alphabetical order (for example, C-D-E-F-G-A-B-C).

Scale Degree Names: Tonic (I), Supertonic (ii), Mediant (iii), Subdominant (IV), Dominant (V), Submediant (vi), Leading Tone (vii^o).

Second Inversion: A triad written with the fifth as the lowest note. The figured bass symbol for a triad in second inversion is 6/4. The figured bass symbol for a seventh chord in second inversion is 6/4/3, or 4/3.

Secondary Dominant: The V or Dominant of a key other than Tonic (I).

Secondary Triads: The ii, iii, vi, and vii^o chords. (In harmonic minor, ii^o, III$^+$, VI, and vii^o).

Third Inversion: A seventh chord written with the seventh as the lowest note. The figured bass symbol for third inversion is 6/4/2, or 2.

Triad: A chord which contains three different notes, with qualities of Major, minor, Augmented, or diminished.

Whole Tone Scale: A scale made up entirely of whole steps.

Ionian mode: scale in which half steps occur between notes 3-4 and 7-8, like the major scale.

Dorian mode: scale in which half steps occur between notes 2-3 and 6-7, as if playing all white keys from D to D.

Phrygian mode: scale in which half steps occur between notes 1-2 and 5-6, as if playing all white keys from E to E.

Lydian mode: scale in which half steps occur between notes 4-5 and 7-8, as if playing all white keys from F to F.

Mixolydian mode: scale in which half steps occur between notes 3-4 and 6-7, as if playing all white keys from G to G.

Aeolian mode: scale in which half steps occur between notes 2-3 and 5-6, as if playing all white keys from A to A.

Locrian mode: scale in which half steps occur between notes 1-2 and 4-5, as if playing all white keys from B to B.

Pivot chord: A chord that precedes a key change **(modulation)**, and is common to both the original key and the key to which the music changes.

REVIEW
LESSONS 1-10

1. Name these Major keys.

2. Name these minor keys.

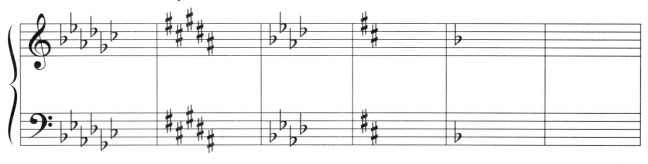

3. Write the key signatures for these keys, in both clefs.

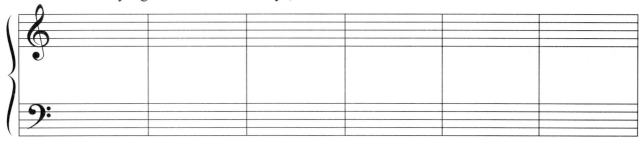

Gb Major   bb minor   c minor   E Major   c# minor   G Major

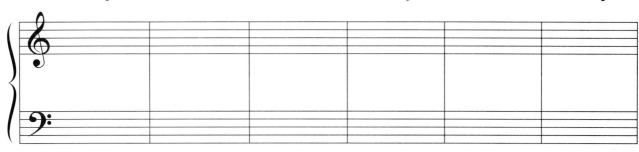

F# Major   e minor   Db Major   Bb Major   A Major   f# minor

4. Write these scales.

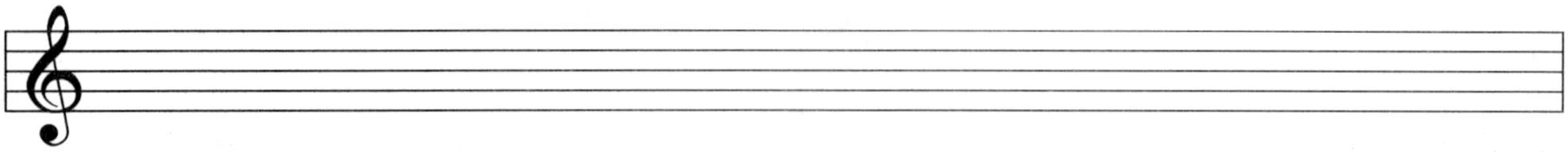

A♭ Major

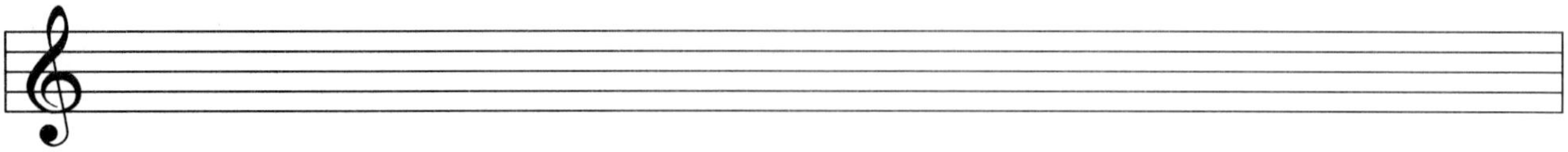

f natural minor

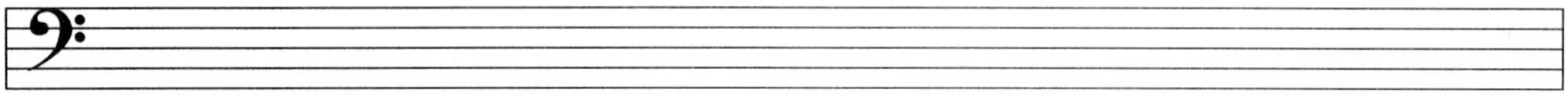

c♯ melodic minor (ascending and descending)

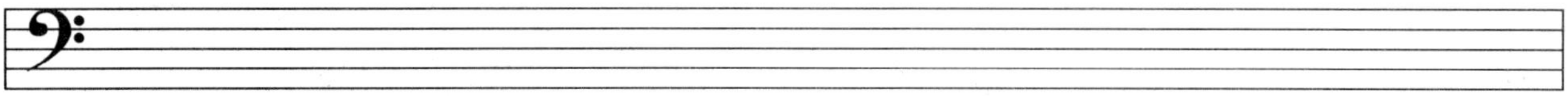

Whole Tone Scale beginning on A

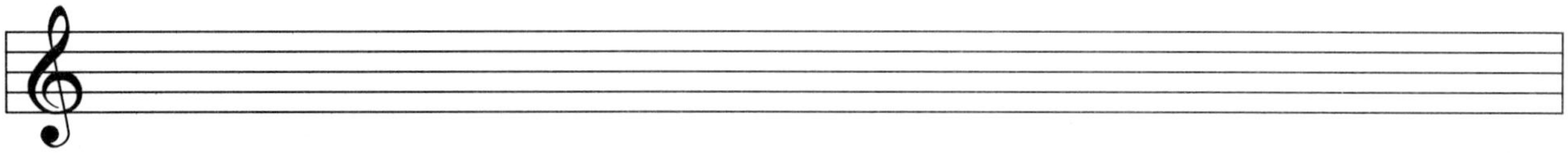

f♯ harmonic minor

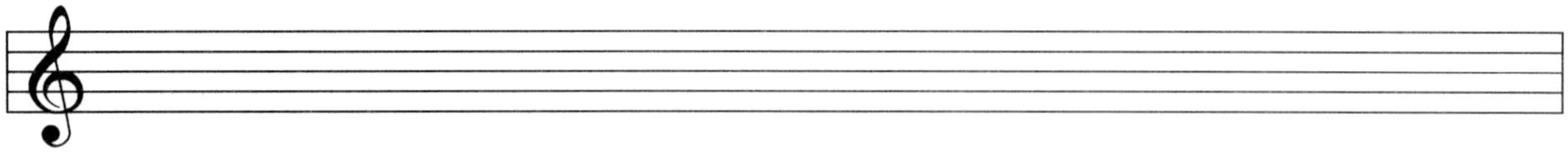

Chromatic Scale beginning on D (ascending and descending)

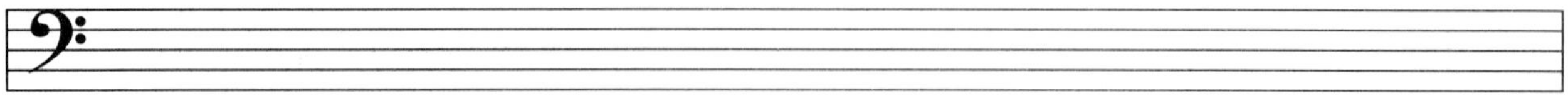

Ionian mode beginning on G

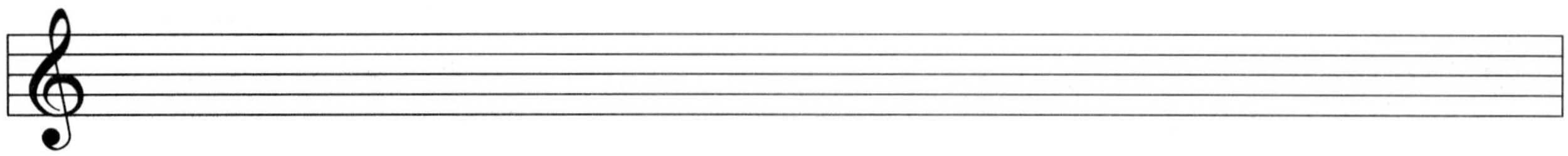

Phrygian mode beginning on E

5. Give the letter name and type of scale used in each of the following melodies.

a. _____ _____

b. _____ _____

c. _____ _____

d. _____ _____

e. _____ _____

f. _____ _____

6. Name these intervals.

_____ _____ _____ _____ _____ _____ _____ _____

7. Complete these intervals. Do not change the given note.

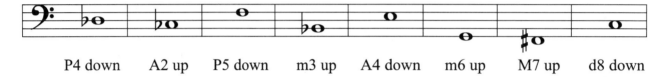

P4 down   A2 up   P5 down   m3 up   A4 down   m6 up   M7 up   d8 down

8. Write diatonic half steps above these notes.

9. Write chromatic half steps above each of these notes.

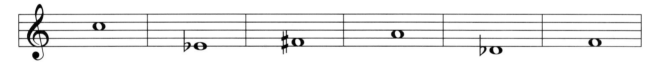

10. Label these triads with their roots, qualities, and figured bass.

_____ _____ _____ _____ _____ _____

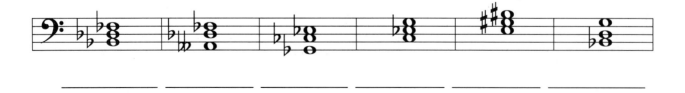

_____ _____ _____ _____ _____ _____

11. Write these triads.

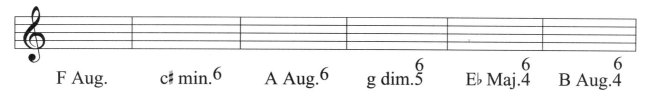

F Aug.   c♯ min.⁶   A Aug.⁶   g dim.⁶₅   E♭ Maj.⁶₄   B Aug.⁶₄

12. Write the scale degree names for the following Roman Numerals.

   a. I or i _____   e. V   _____
   b. ii or ii° _____   f. V⁷   _____
   c. iii or III⁺ _____ g. vi or VI _____
   d. IV or iv _____   h. vii°   _____

13. Write the following chords.

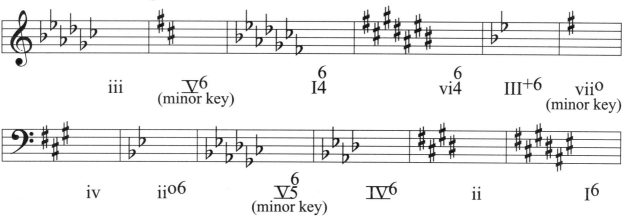

iii   V⁶ (minor key)   I⁶₄   vi⁶₄   III⁺⁶   vii° (minor key)

iv   ii°⁶   V⁶₅ (minor key)   IV⁶   ii   I⁶

14. Write these cadences.

V⁷ I   V VI   IV I   i V

15. Write these chord progressions.

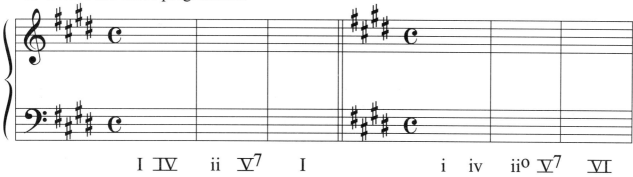

I IV ii V⁷ I   i iv ii° V⁷ VI

16. The following example is from Mazurka, Op. 67, No. 4, by Chopin. Answer the questions about the music.

a. What is the key or tonality? _____ _____

b. Name the circled intervals.

1. _____ 2. _____ 3. _____ 4. _____ 5. _____ 6. _____ 7. _____

c. Give the letter name, quality, Roman Numeral, and figured bass (inversion) for each boxed chord.

	LETTER	**QUALITY**	**ROMAN NUMERAL AND FIGURED BASS**
Chord a:	_____	_____	_____
Chord b:	_____	_____	_____
Chord c:	_____	_____	_____
Chord d:	_____	_____	_____ of _____
Chord e:	_____	_____	_____

d. What is the term for chord d? _____ _____

e. To what key does the example modulate? _____

17. The following example is from *New Year's Eve* by Schumann. Answer the questions about the music.

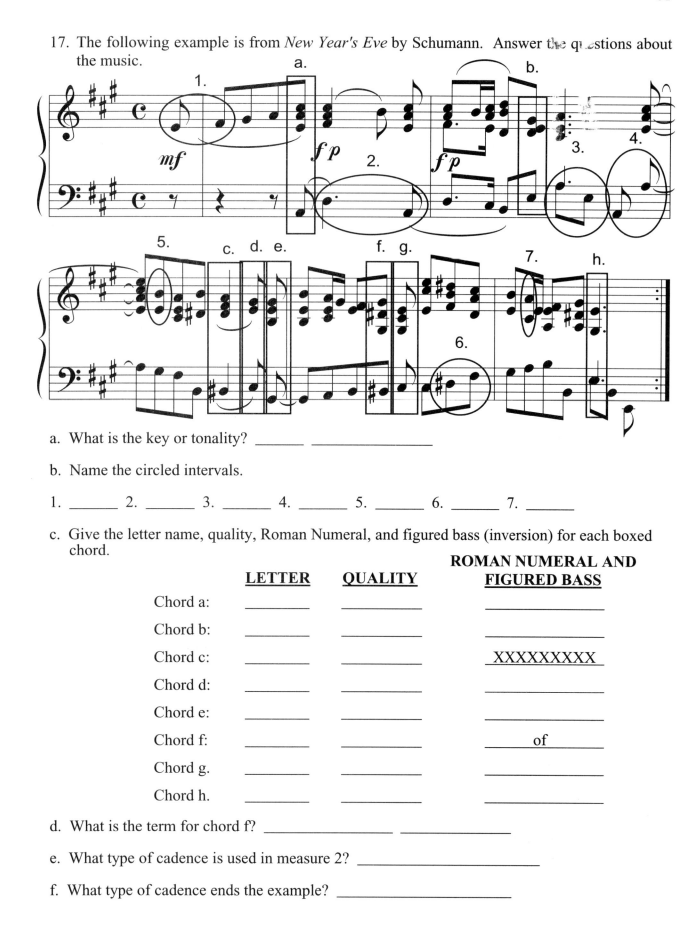

a. What is the key or tonality? _____ _____

b. Name the circled intervals.

1. _____ 2. _____ 3. _____ 4. _____ 5. _____ 6. _____ 7. _____

c. Give the letter name, quality, Roman Numeral, and figured bass (inversion) for each boxed chord.

	LETTER	QUALITY	ROMAN NUMERAL AND FIGURED BASS
Chord a:	_____	_____	_____
Chord b:	_____	_____	_____
Chord c:	_____	_____	XXXXXXXXX
Chord d:	_____	_____	_____
Chord e:	_____	_____	_____
Chord f:	_____	_____	_____ of _____
Chord g.	_____	_____	_____
Chord h.	_____	_____	_____

d. What is the term for chord f? _____ _____

e. What type of cadence is used in measure 2? _____

f. What type of cadence ends the example? _____

18. The following example is from *French Suite No. VI: Gavotte,* by J.S. Bach. Answer the questions about the music.

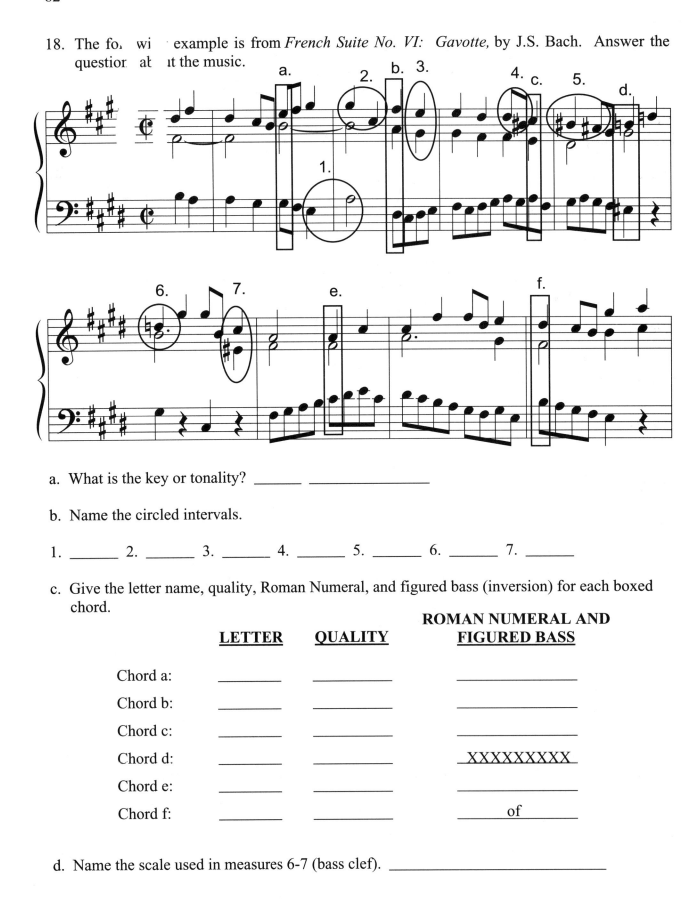

a. What is the key or tonality? _____ _____

b. Name the circled intervals.

1. _____ 2. _____ 3. _____ 4. _____ 5. _____ 6. _____ 7. _____

c. Give the letter name, quality, Roman Numeral, and figured bass (inversion) for each boxed chord.

	LETTER	**QUALITY**	**ROMAN NUMERAL AND FIGURED BASS**
Chord a:	_____	_____	_____
Chord b:	_____	_____	_____
Chord c:	_____	_____	_____
Chord d:	_____	_____	XXXXXXXXX
Chord e:	_____	_____	_____
Chord f:	_____	_____	_____ of _____

d. Name the scale used in measures 6-7 (bass clef). _____

LESSON 11
TIME SIGNATURES

The **TIME SIGNATURE** for a composition is found at the beginning of the music, next to the key signature. The time signature is often made up of two numbers:

Sometimes, the symbol 𝄴 or 𝄵 is used instead of numbers.

𝄴 stands for $\frac{4}{4}$, or **Common Time.**

𝄵 stands for $\frac{2}{2}$, or **Alla Breve.**

The **top** number of the time signature tells **how many beats each measure contains.**

The **bottom** number tells **which type of note receives one beat.**

$\begin{matrix}2\\4\end{matrix}$ = 2 beats per measure
= Quarter note (♩) receives one beat

$\begin{matrix}3\\8\end{matrix}$ = 3 beats per measure
= Eighth note (♪) receives one beat

METER is determined by the time signature, and refers to the division of beats into equal groups, such as groups of three beats for a piece of music in $\frac{3}{4}$ time.

When the bottom number of a time signature is a "4," a quarter note (♩) receives one beat or count. The following chart shows how many beats to give these notes or rests (other types of counting are possible):

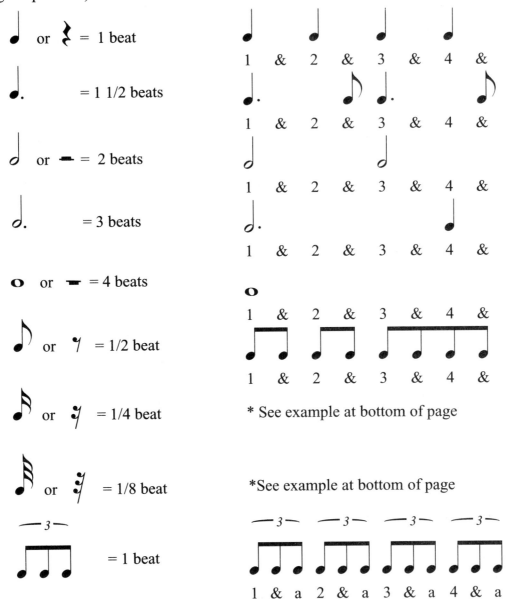

* Counting for some of the more common eighth, sixteenth, and thirty-second note patterns is shown here:

An **UPBEAT** occurs when an incomplete measure begins the piece. The last beat or beats are "borrowed" from the final measure of the piece and placed at the beginning. The beats used for the upbeat measure will be the last numbers of the time signature. The final measure will have fewer beats than normal. The first full measure begins with count number 1.

Example:

When the bottom number of a time signature is a "2," a half note (♩) receives one beat or count. The following chart shows how many beats to give these notes or rests:

♩ or 𝄼	= 1 beat
♩.	= 1 1/2 beats
𝅝 or 𝄻	= 2 beats
♩ or 𝄽	= 1/2 beat
♪ or 𝄾	= 1/4 beat
♪ or 𝄿	= 1/8 beat
♪ or 𝅀	= 1/16 beat

When the bottom number of a time signature is an 8, an eighth note (♪) receives one beat.

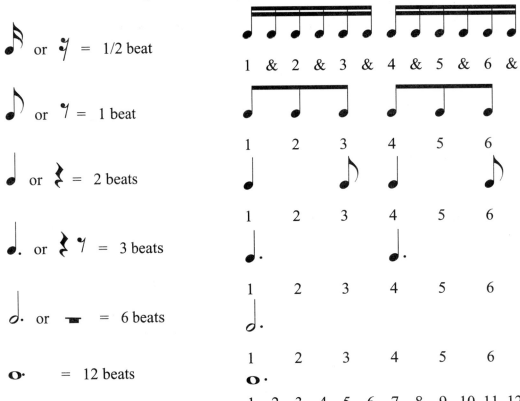

1. Fill in the blanks. (The first one is done for you.)

2/4 = 2 beats per measure
= Quarter note receives one beat or count

3/4 = _____
= _____

3/8 = _____
= _____

C = _____

¢ = _____

2/2 = _____
= _____

7/4 = _____
= _____

6/8 = _____

When a time signature has a 2 on top (2/2, 2/4, etc.), the first beat of the measure is strongest. There are two pulses per measure.

When a time signature has a 3 on top (3/8, 3/4, etc.), the first beat of the measure is strongest. There are three pulses per measure.

When a time signature has a 4 on top (4/2, 4/4, etc.), the first beat of the measure is strongest, and the third beat is also a strong beat. There are four pulses per measure.

When a time signature has a 6 on top (6/8, 6/4, etc.), the first beat of the measure is strongest, and the fourth beat is also a strong beat. There are **two large pulses** per measure, each containing three smaller beats.

When a time signature has a 9 on top (9/8, 9/4, etc.), the first beat of each measure is strongest, and the fourth and seventh beats are also strong beats. There are **three large pulses** per measure, each containing three smaller beats.

When a time signature has a 12 on top (12/8, 12/4, etc.), the first beat of each measure is strongest, and the fourth, seventh, and tenth beats are also strong beats. There are **four large pulses** per measure, each containing three smaller beats.

Syncopation occurs when there is a strong note on a weak beat. The syncopations are circled in the example below.

When a time signature has a 5 or 7 on top, the accented beats are irregular. Music which is in 5/4, 5/8, etc., will be divided into groups of 2 + 3 or 3 + 2. Music which is in 7/4, 7/8, etc., will be divided into groups of 4 + 3 or 3 + 4.

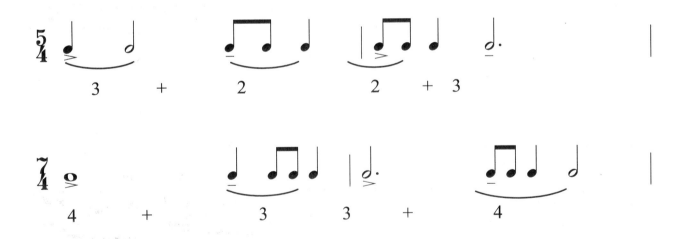

Note: The accents above are only intended to demonstrate where strong and weak beats occur within the given meter. They are not meant to imply that every strong beat receives an accent.

2. Write the counts for these phrases, and place accents on the strong beats. Tell how many pulses will be in each measure.

   a. From *Bunte Blatter, Op. 99, No. III,* by Schumann. _____ pulses per measure

   b. From *La fille aux cheveux de lin,* by Debussy. _____ pulses per measure

   c. From *Invention No. 3* by J.S. Bach. _____ pulses per measure

d. From *Kinderscenen, Op. 15, no. 6,* by Schumann. _____ pulses per measure

e. From *Sonata, Op. 49, No. 1,* by Beethoven. _____ pulses per measure

f. From *Bagatelle No. 2* by Tcherepnin. _____ pulses per measure

g. From *Sonatina, 1959,* by Khachaturian. _____ pulses per measure

h. From *Little Fugue* by Schumann. _____ pulses per measure

i. From *Sonatina, 1959,* by Khachaturian. _____ pulses per measure

j. From *Gathering of the Grapes--Happy Time!* by Schumann. _____ pulses per measure

k. From *Waltz, Op. posth. 69, No. 1,* by Chopin. _____ pulses per measure

l. From *Nocturne in c# minor* by Chopin. _____ pulses per measure

LESSON 12
SIGNS AND TERMS

Music often contains signs and terms other than notes and rhythms. Memorize the ones listed below.

A Tempo: Return to the original tempo (the speed at which the piece began).

Accent: Play the note louder than the others.

Accelerando: Accelerate; gradually faster.

Adagio: Slowly.

Allargando: Broadening; gradually slower.

Allegro: Fast or quick.

Allegretto: Slighly slower than Allegro; faster than Andante.

Andante: A moderate walking tempo.

Andantino: Slightly faster than Andante. (Some composers use it to mean slower than Andante).

Animato: Animated; with spirit.

 Appoggiatura: Used mainly in music of the Classical Period (see Lesson 17), play the first note as half the value of the second note:

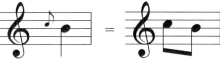

Arpeggio: A continuous broken chord:

Atonality: No specific key or tonality.

Bitonality: The use of two different keys at the same time.

Canon: A strict form of contrapuntal writing in which each voice exactly imitates the melody of the first voice.

Cantabile: In a singing style.

Coda: An extended ending for a piece of music.

Codetta: A short Coda.

Con: With.

Con Brio: With vigor or spirit (with brilliance).

Con Fuoco: With fire or fury.

Con Moto: With motion.

Crescendo: Gradually louder.

D.C. al Fine: Go back to the beginning of the piece, and play until the word *Fine* (which means end).

Damper Pedal: Press the pedal located on the right.

Decrescendo or Diminuendo: Gradually softer.

Dolce: Sweetly.

Doloroso: Sadly; sorrowfully.

Double Flat: Two flats placed before a note, indicating to lower the note a whole step.

B double flat is played as A on the piano

Double Sharp: The symbol 𝄪 placed before a note, indicating to raise the note a whole step.

G double sharp is played as A on the piano.

Dynamics: Letters or symbols which tell how loudly or softly to play the music.

Enharmonic: Two different names for the same pitch, such as C♯ and D♭.

Espressivo: Expressively.

Fine: The end.

f **Forte:** Loud.

ff **Fortissimo:** Very loud.

fff **Fortississimo:** Very, very loud.

fp **Forte-piano:** Loud followed immediately by soft.

⌒ **Fermata:** Hold the note longer than its value.

 **First and Second Ending:** Play the piece with the first ending (under the 1.), then repeat the piece. The second time through, skip the first ending and play the second ending (under the 2.).

Giocoso: Merrily, with humor.

Gracioso: Gracefully.

Largo: Very slowly; "large."

 **Legato Sign (slur):** Play smoothly; connect the notes.

Leggiero: lightly, delicately.

Lento: Slowly.

m.d. *mano destra;* use the right hand.

m.s.: *mano sinistra;* use the left hand.

Marcato: Stressed, marked.

Meno: Less.

Meno mosso: Less motion; slower.

mf **Mezzo Forte:** Medium loud.

mp **Mezzo Piano:** Medium soft.

Moderato: A moderate or medium tempo.

Molto: Much; very.

 **Mordent:** An ornament in which the written note is played, followed by the note below the written note and the written note again:

 **Octave Sign (8va):** Play the notes an octave higher (or lower if below the notes) than where they are written.

Opus: A word used to indicate the chronological order in which a composer's music was written.

Ostinato: A repeated pattern, such as:

Parallel Major/minor: Major and minor keys with the same letter names (such as C Major and c minor).

p **Piano:** Soft.

pp **Pianissimo:** Very soft.

ppp **Pianississimo:** Very, very soft.

Pesante: Heavily.

Phrase: A musical sentence, often four measures long.

Piu: More.

Piu Mosso: More motion; faster.

Poco: Little.

Polytonality: The use of several different keys at the same time.

Presto: Very fast.

Rallentando: Gradually slower.

Relative Major /minor: Major and minor keys which have the same key signature.

‖: :‖ **Repeat Sign:** Repeat the previous sections of music. Go back to the nearest repeat sign, or to the beginning of the piece if there is none.

Ritardando (*ritard., rit.,*): Slow down gradually.

Ritenuto: Immediately slower.

Robusto: Robustly, boldly.

Scherzando: Playfully, jokingly.

Sempre: Always.

Senza: Without.

Sforzando: A sudden, sharp accent.

Simile: Continue in the same style.

 Slur: Connect the notes; play smoothly.

Spiritoso: Spirited; with spirit.

Sostenuto: Sustained.

Staccato: Play crisply or detached.

Subito: Suddenly; at once.

Syncopation: A momentary contradiction of the meter or pulse, often by changing strong and weak beats within a measure. For example:

Tempo: The speed at which to play the music.

Tenuto Play the note slightly louder than the others; stress the note. May also mean to give the note its full value.

 **Tie:** Hold the second note; do not play it.

Tranquillo: Tranquilly, peacefully, calmly.

Tre Corde: Release the Una Corda pedal (soft pedal; left pedal).

 **Trill:** An ornament in which the written note is alternated with the note above:

Baroque or Classical Period: begin on the note above the written note.

Romantic Period: begin on the written note.

 **Trill with prefix:** A trill performed with an added beginning from above or below:

 **Turn:** An ornament in which the written note is surrounded by its upper and lower neighbors:

Una Corda: Often abbreviated U.C. in music. Press the left or soft pedal.

Vivace: Quick, lively.

Vivo: Brisk, lively.

...etto: A suffix meaning little or less than, such as Allegretto for a little slower than Allegro.

...ino: A suffix meaning little or less than, such as Andantino for a little faster than Andante.

1. Match these terms and symbols with their definitions.

_____ *ff*   a. Mezzo Piano: Medium soft

_____ *fff*   b. Pianissimo: Very soft

_____ *sfz*   c. Piano: Soft

_____ *f*   d. Fortissimo: Very loud

_____ *pp*   e. Mezzo Forte: Medium loud

_____ 8va   f. Symbols that indicate loud or soft

_____ Dynamics   g. Forte: Loud

_____ *mp*   h. Play one octave higher

_____ *mf*   i. Fortississimo: Very, very loud

_____ *ppp*   j. Sforzando: A sudden, sharp accent

_____ *p*   k. Pianississimo: Very, very soft

2. Match these terms and symbols with their definitions.

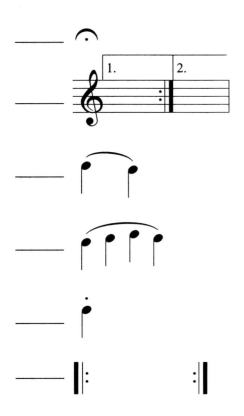

a. Legato: Connect the notes

b. Repeat sign: repeat the music

c. Staccato: Crisply or detached (not connected)

d. Slur: Connect the notes; play smoothly

e. Fermata: Hold the note longer than its value

f. First and Second Ending

3. Match these terms and symbols with their definitions.

_____ (tenuto note)

_____ Ped. ✽ |_____|

_____ Phrase

_____ (accent note)

_____ D. C. al Fine

_____ Ritardando (*rit.*)

_____ A Tempo

a. Use the damper pedal (the pedal on the right)

b. A musical sentence, often four measures long

c. Stress or tenuto: Stress the note, or play it slightly louder than the others

d. Accent: Play the note louder than the others

e. Slow down gradually

f. Return to the original tempo (the speed with which you began the music)

g. Go back to the beginning and play until you see the word "*Fine*"

4. Match these terms and symbols with their definitions.

_____ Allegro   a. Walking tempo

_____ Andante   b. Gradually louder

_____ Moderato   c. Slow down gradually

_____ Vivace   d. Gradually softer

_____ >   e. Slowly

_____ <   f. A moderate or medium tempo

_____ Adagio   g. Quick or lively

_____ Lento   h. With brilliance

_____ Rallentando   i. Fast, quick

_____ Con Brio   j. Slowly

5. Match these terms and symbols with their definitions.

_____ *fp*   a. Sadly, sorrowfully

_____ Scherzando   b. Boldly, robustly

_____ Doloroso   c. More

_____ Opus   d. Heavily

_____ Robusto   e. Sustained

_____ Piu   f. Playfully, jokingly

_____ Pesante   g. System of classifying a composer's works chronologically

_____ Sostenuto   h. Loud, followed immediately by soft

6. Match these terms and symbols with their definitions.

_____ Andantino

_____ Con Moto

_____ Dolce

_____ [appoggiatura symbol]

_____ Accelerando

_____ [trill symbol]

_____ Una Corda

_____ Cantabile

_____ Molto

_____ [turn symbol]

_____ [mordent symbol]

_____ Codetta

_____ Poco

_____ Tre Corde

_____ Spiritoso

_____ [trill with prefix symbol]

_____ Coda

_____ Sempre

_____ [trill with prefix symbol]

a. Trill: [notation]

b. Gradually faster

c. Trill with prefix: [notation]

d. Use soft pedal (left pedal)

e. Slightly faster than Andante

f. Sweetly

g. With Motion

h. With Spirit

i. Little

j. Much, greatly

k. A short coda

l. Release the soft pedal (left pedal)

m. Trill with prefix: [notation]

n. In a singing style

o. Mordent: [notation]

p. An extended ending

q. Appoggiatura: [notation]

r. Always

s. Turn: [notation]

7. Match these terms and symbols with their definitions.

_____ Presto   a. Expressively

_____ Vivo   b. Without

_____ Espressivo   c. Suddenly; at once

_____ Leggiero   d. Very fast

_____ Senza   e. Stressed; marked

_____ Marcato   f. Brisk, lively

_____ Subito   g. Continue in the same style

_____ Simile   h. Lightly; delicately

8. Match these terms and symbols with their definitions.

_____ Largo   a. Animated; with spirit

_____ Giocoso   b. Gracefully

_____ Animato   c. With fire

_____ Bitonality   d. No specific key or tonality

_____ Allegretto   e. Peacefully; calmly; tranquilly

_____ Grazioso   f. Merrily; with humor

_____ Con Fuoco   g. The use of two different keys at the same time

_____ Atonality   h. Slightly slower than Allegro

_____ Polytonality   i. Very slowly; "large"

_____ Tranquillo   j. The use of several different keys at the same time

9. Match these terms and symbols with their definitions.

_____ Allargando

_____ ...etto

_____ ...ino

_____ Meno

_____ Canon

_____ Ritenuto

_____ Enharmonic

_____ Parallel Major and minor

_____ Relative Major and minor

_____ Meno mosso

_____ Piu mosso

_____ Syncopation

_____ Arpeggio

_____ Ostinato

_____ Double Flat

_____ Double Sharp

_____ m.d., *mano destra*

_____ m.s., *mano sinistra*

a. Two names for the same pitch

b. Broadening, gradually slower

c. Little

d. Less motion

e. Less

f. Strong notes on weak beats

g. Major and minor keys with the same key signature

h. Immediately slower

i. Little

j. A strict form of contrapuntal writing in which each voice exactly imitates the melody of the first voice

k. More motion

l. Major and minor keys with the same letter names

m. Use right hand

n. A continuous broken chord

o. Raise the note a whole step

p. Use left hand

q. Lower the note a whole step

r. A repeated pattern

LESSON 13
COMPOSITIONAL TECHNIQUES

A **MOTIVE** is a short group of notes used in a piece of music. The composer uses this motive as the main idea of the music and repeats it in many different ways.

A **THEME** is an entire phrase of music, which is the basis of the composition. (A composition may have more than one theme.)

Beethoven's *Symphony No. 5* uses this **motive:**

It is repeated, with variations, several times at the beginning of the symphony, to create the **theme:**

It would be helpful to listen to the entire first movement of Beethoven's *Symphony No. 5*, and you will hear its motive and theme used in many interesting ways.

REPETITION takes place when the motive is repeated immediately, exactly the way it was the first time it occurred, on the same note.

This example, from *Waltz, Op. 69, No. 1* by Chopin, uses repetition. The repetition is circled.

SEQUENCE occurs when the motive is repeated immediately, on a different note, usually a 2nd or 3rd higher or lower.

This example, from *French Suite No. II: Courante* by J.S. Bach, uses sequence. The sequence is circled.

IMITATION occurs when the motive is repeated immediately in another voice, such as in the bass clef following a statement of the motive in the treble clef.

This example, from *Invention No. 3* by J.S. Bach, uses imitation. The imitation is circled.

CANON occurs when the entire **theme** is repeated in another voice. The difference between imitation and canon is that imitation uses only a motive, while canon is a strict copy of the entire theme.

Dona Nobis Pacem shows the use of canon. Notice how the bass clef part copies the entire theme which was introduced in the treble clef.

PEDAL POINT or **ORGAN POINT** occurs when there is a sustained or repeated note, usually in the bass (although sometimes in higher voices), which stays for some time while the other voices continue to change harmonies.

This example, from *Invention No. 4* by J.S. Bach, shows the use of pedal or organ point.

AUGMENTATION is the exact doubling of the rhythmic value of the notes within a theme (for example, the quarter notes become half notes).

DIMINUTION occurs when the rhythmic values of a theme are divided in half (for example, quarter notes become eighth notes).

1. Circle the repetition, imitation, sequence, canon, pedal point, augmentation, or diminution in each example below, then write the type of compositional technique on the line above the music.

a. From *Variations on Ah! Vous dirai-je,* by Mozart. _____

b. From *Invention No. 3* by J.S. Bach. _____

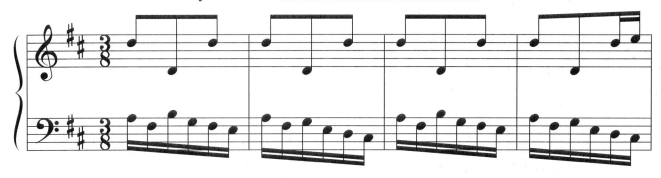

c. From *Invention No. 4* by J.S. Bach. _____

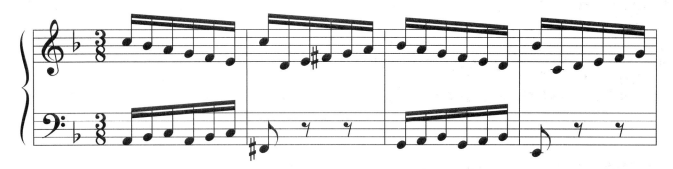

d. From *Invention No. 4* by J.S. Bach. _____

e. From *Song of War* by Schumann. _____

f. Original.

g. Original

h. From *Little Fugue* by Schumann.

i. From *Bunte Blatter, Op. 99, No. 3,* by Schumann. _____

j. Original _____

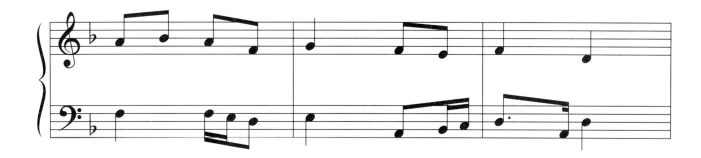

k. From *Little Canon* by Schumann. _____

l. From *Mazurka, Op. 67, No. 4,* by Chopin. _____

m. Original _____

LESSON 14
HOMOPHONIC AND POLYPHONIC TEXTURES

TEXTURE is the manner in which the various voices or parts of music relate to one another; how the voices are put together.

POLYPHONIC TEXTURE occurs when there are two or more parts which are of equal importance. The melodies are passed between the voices. This example, from *Invention No. 3* by J.S. Bach, shows the use of polyphonic texture.

HOMOPHONIC TEXTURE occurs when there is one voice which dominates the music, while the other voice or voices serve as an accompaniment. Homophonic texture may either be **chordal** in nature, or may have a **separate melody and accompaniment.** This example, from *Mazurka, Op. 67, No. 4,* by Chopin, shows the use of homophonic texture.*

*Some theory scholars divide texture into three categories: polyphonic (or contrapuntal), homophonic (melody and accompaniment), and chordal.

1. Name the texture of each example below.

a. From *Invention No. 8* by J.S. Bach. _____ texture

b. From *Song of War* by Schumann. _____ texture

c. From *Sonata, Op. 49, No. 1,* by Beethoven. _____ texture

d. From *Little Canon* by Schumann. _____ texture

e. From *Kinderscenen, Op. 15, No. 6,* by Schumann. _____ texture

f. From *Little Fugue* by Schumann. _____ texture

LESSON 15
TRANSPOSITION

TRANSPOSITION occurs when a piece of music is played or written in a key that is different from the original.

For example, the first version of "Frere Jacques" below (Example A) is in the key of C Major. The second version (Example B) is in G Major. The piece has been transposed from C Major to G Major.

Notice how the intervals remain the same in both versions, and if played, the melody sounds the same, but higher in pitch.

EXAMPLE A: FRERE JACQUES in the key of C Major

EXAMPLE B: FRERE JACQUES in the key of G Major

Follow these steps when transposing a melody:

1. Determine the key of the original melody.

2. Determine the key signature of the key to which the music will be transposed.

3. Look at the first note of the original melody and determine its scale degree or its place in the scale. For example, if the original key is C Major and the melody begins on G, the starting note is the 5th.

4. The first note for the new key will be the same interval above the new tonic as the original. For example, when the new key is D Major and the starting note was a 5th above tonic, the new starting note will be A, a 5th above D.

5. Continue writing the transposition by determining each interval of the original melody and using that interval for the new melody. Add any necessary sharps or flats.

6. Check your progress by following steps 3 and 4 for any given note.

Example: Mary Had a Little Lamb, transposed from C Major to G Major.

1. Original key: C Major.

2. New key signature for G Major: F#.

3. First note of original is E, the 3rd note of G Major

4. Starting note will be B, the 3rd note of G Major.

5. Melody moves up and down by seconds and thirds. See examples below.

MARY HAD A LITTLE LAMB in C Major

MARY HAD A LITTLE LAMB in G Major

Another way to transpose a melody is to move each note up or down the same distance. In the example of "Mary Had a Little Lamb" above, each note would be raised a Perfect 5th. The first E becomes B, the D becomes A, the C becomes G, etc.

1. Transpose this example (from *Hungarian Folk Song* by Bartok) to the key of G Major. Write the transposition on the blank staff below the example.

2. Transpose this example (from *Sonatina, Op. 36, No. 1,* by Clementi) to the key of B♭ Major. Write the transposition on the blank staff below the music.

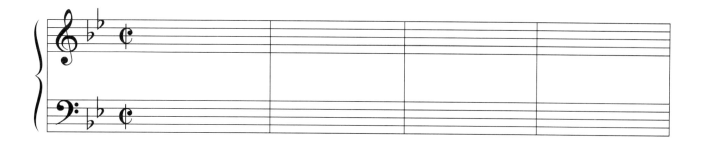

This page has purposely been left blank

LESSON 16
THE FOUR PERIODS OF MUSIC HISTORY
THE BAROQUE PERIOD
KIRNBERGER, TELEMANN, AND VIVALDI

The history of music since 1600 is divided into four periods:

Baroque: 1600-1750

Classical: 1750-1830

Romantic: 1830-1900

Contemporary: 1900-present
Currently, there is not a definitive division of years for the 20th and 21st centuries. Many historians now place the Contemporary Period later, beginning after 1950 or 1960. This period can also be called "Modern" or "Post-Common Practice." Yet another division is the 20th Century (1900-1999), and the Contemporary Period (2000-Present).

Music of the **BAROQUE PERIOD** (1600-1750) is characterized by the following:

a. **Polyphonic Texture:** Two or more separate voices are interchanged to create the music. The melodies are passed between the parts, and the parts are of equal importance.

b. **Use of Ornamentation:** Composers included many trills, mordents, and other ornaments in their music. It was the performer's responsibility to know how to play the ornaments correctly. Performers could also add their own ornaments at appropriate places in the music.

c. **Improvisation:** Not only did music of the Baroque Period contain many ornaments, the performer was also free to improvise sections of the music. This not only included adding the ornaments mentioned above, but also playing **Cadenzas,** entire sections of music that the performer created, often after a cadence in the music.

Another type of improvisation in Baroque music was the use of **Figured Bass.** The performer was given an outline of the chord progression of a composition. The performer improvised using the harmonies specified by the figured bass.

FIGURED BASS

d. **Dance Suite:** Works which include many different dances, performed together. Typical Baroque dance suites include these dances, in this order:

Allemande: A dance in moderate 4/4 time with a short upbeat, often using short running figures that are passed through a semi-contrapuntal texture.

Courante or Corrente: A Courante is a French dance in moderate 3/2 or 6/4 time, which shifts from one of these meters to the other. The texture is free counterpoint, with a shifting melody. A Corrente is an Italian dance in quick triple meter, with continuous running figures, and homophonic texture.

Sarabande: A dance in slow triple meter and dignified style, often with an accented or long tone on the second beat. It probably originated in Mexico as a wild dance, but as it moved to France and England its style became calm and dignified.

Optional Dances: Minuet: A French country dance in 3/4 meter.
Bouree: A French dance, usually in quick duple meter with a single upbeat.
Gavotte: A French dance in moderate 4/4 time, with an upbeat of two quarter notes, and with phrases usually beginning and ending in the middle of the measure.
Passapeid: A spirited dance in quick 3/8 or 6/8 meter, possibly originating in Brittany.
Polonaise: A Polish dance of stately and festive character, in moderate triple meter. It often contains measures with a short repeated rhythmic motive.
Anglaise: A dance in fast duple meter, derived from the English country dance.
Loure: From the 16th and 17th century term for bagpipe, this dance is in moderate 6/4 time, with dotted rhythms and heavy downbeats.
Air: A song, rather than a dance, with melodic characteristics.

Gigue Originated from English Jigs, the French Gigue is in compound duple meter (6/8, for example), contains dotted rhythms and large intervals (6ths, 7ths), and has fugal (canon-like) texture. The Italian Giga is quicker, non fugal, and has running passages over a harmonic bass. These are more rare in Baroque suites than the French Gigue.

e. Most keyboard music of the Baroque Period was written for the **harpsichord, clavichord,** and **organ**. The piano was not invented and perfected until late in the Baroque Period.

f. **Terraced Dynamics:** Since much of the keyboard music from the Baroque Period was written for the harpsichord, which does not have the capability of making crescendos or diminuendos, performers used terraced dynamics. This takes place when the dynamics increase or decrease by sections: p mp mf f, rather than gradually. (This type of dynamic contrast is most prevelant in keyboard music of the period. Other instruments, such as the violin, did create true crescendos and decrescendos during the Baroque Period.)

This example, from *Short Prelude No. 7* by J.S. Bach, shows these characteristics: Polyphonic texture and terraced dynamics.

JOHANN PHILIPP KIRNBERGER

Johann Philipp Kirnberger lived during the Baroque Period. He was born in Germany in 1721. Kirnberger studied violin and harpsichord in his local area until 1739, when (at age 18) he studied with J.S. Bach. His jobs after that included working for various Polish noblemen, music director at the Benedictine Convent in Reusch-Lembert, violinist at the Prussian royal chapel, a job at the chapel of Prince Heinrich of Prussia, and finally working for Princess Anna Analia of Prussia.

While Kirnberger did write a fair amount of music, including solo instrumental music, chamber music, and vocal works, he is mainly known for his contributions as a theorist. He wrote many theoretical works, and was highly regarded as a teacher, having taught the well known musician, J.A.P. Schultz.

Kirnberger died in Berlin in July of 1783.

GEORG PHILIPP TELEMANN

Georg Philipp Telemann was another Baroque composer, born in 1681 in Germany. He taught himself as a child by studying the works of other composers, and at age twelve wrote his first opera. He began studying law at Leipzig University, but switched to music study. He held a number of positions, which included organist and director of the Neukirche in Leipzig, musical director of the Leipzig Opera, Kappelmeister of court of Sorau (in present-day Poland), Kappelmeister at the Barfusserkirche in Frankfurt, and finally musical director and Kantor in Hamburg.

His vocal works include several operas, oratorios, secular cantatas, serenades, Passions, sacred cantatas, odes, chorales, sacred canons, Masses, psalms, and motets. He wrote an overwhelming amount of instrumental music as well, including orchestral works, chamber music, duos, trios, and a large amount of keyboard music. During his lifetime, Telemann was considered the leading German composer, being more highly regarded than J.S. Bach. His style was influenced by many different countries, and his music had appeal to the general public as it was written to meet the needs not only of professional musicians, but also those of amateurs. He had a true concern for music for the masses, exhibited by his attempts to create musical societies in the cities where he worked.

After Telemann's death in 1767, his music was largely forgotten. In recent years, however, interest in his music has grown. He may have written more music than any other composer in the history of music.

ANTONIO VIVALDI

Antonio Vivaldi is yet another Baroque composer, born in Italy in 1678, and a son of a violinist. He was a priest, but almost immediately upon receiving his full priesthood, he had to quit saying Mass because of an illness. He then became a teacher at an orphanage for girls which had special emphasis in music education, and an excellent choir and orchestra. He taught violin, and composed a great deal of music for the girls to perform. He later went to work for the governor of Mantua, and spent several years in Rome, while at the same time returning to Venice frequently to write and direct operas.

Vivaldi made important contributions to the development of violin playing and to the concerto. He was well known for his virtuosity as a performer, and his compositions include many of the techniques for which he was admired. His 500 or so concertos were more like those of the Classical Period than those of his Baroque contemporaries. His most popular work is the *Four Seasons,* which is used frequently in today's television shows and movies.

Vivaldi died in Vienna in 1741. Although he earned a great deal of money, he died a poor man, due to his extravagent lifestyle.

Some other well known Baroque composers are:

J.S. Bach, borh in Germany, 1685-1750

Girolamo Frescobaldi, born in Italy, 1583-1643

G.F. Handel, born in Germany, 1685-1760

Henry Purcell, born in England, 1659-1695

Domenico Scarlatti, born in Italy, 1685-1757

Antonio Soler, born in Spain, 1729-1783

1. Name the four periods of music history and give their approximate dates.

   _____   _____

   _____   _____

   _____   _____

   _____   _____

2. List the six characteristics of Baroque music mentioned above, and describe each.

   a. _____

   _____

   _____

   b. _____

   _____

   _____

   c. _____

   _____

   _____

   d. _____

   _____

   _____

   e. _____

   _____

   _____

f. _____

_____

_____

3. Name the movements of a Baroque Dance Suite, and give a brief description of each.

_____

_____

_____

_____

_____

_____

_____

_____

4. Complete the following information about each of these composers.

a. **Johann Philipp Kirnberger**

Dates of birth and death: _____

Historical period: _____

Country of birth: _____

Types of compositions: _____

Positions held: _____

_____

_____

Other contributions to music: _____

_____

b. **Georg Philipp Telemann**

Dates of birth and death: _____

Historical period: _____

Country of birth: _____

Positions held: _____

_____

_____

Types of works: _____

_____

_____

c. **Antonio Vivaldi**

Dates of birth and death: _____

Historical period: _____

Country of birth: _____

Types of compositions: _____

Positions held: _____

_____

_____

Other contributions to music: _____

_____

5. Name six other Baroque composers, their places of birth, and their dates of birth and death.

   _____   _____   _____

   _____   _____   _____

   _____   _____   _____

   _____   _____   _____

   _____   _____   _____

   _____   _____   _____

LESSON 17
THE CLASSICAL PERIOD
CLEMENTI, CZERNY, AND DIABELLI

The **CLASSICAL PERIOD** of music took place from approximately 1750-1830. Music from the Classical Period includes the following characteristics:

a. **Homophonic Texture:** Much of the music of the Classical Period has an obvious melody, with accompaniment.

b. **Cadence points usually obvious:** Quite often, the harmonic structure of Classical music is clear, and the cadences are obvious, both harmonically and by the use of rests at the ends of sections.

c. **Alberti Bass:** A common type of accompaniment for the left hand part of piano music from the Classical Period is Alberti Bass, a repeated pattern in this style:

ALBERTI BASS

e. **Sonata and Sonatina forms:** A sonata or sonatina may contain several movements (usually two, three, or four), with the first movement having an **Exposition, Development**, and **Recapitulation.** When there are three movements, the second is usually a slow movement in a different but related key, and the third is often a Rondo (ABACABA form), in the same key as the first movement.

Sonata Form:	**Exposition**	**Development**	**Recapitulation**
(or Sonata Allegro Form)	Theme 1/Theme 2	Use of themes in	Theme1/Theme2
	Tonic New Key	various keys	Tonic Tonic

This example, from *Sonatina, Op. 36, No. 3* by Clementi, shows these characteristics: Homophonic texture, clear melody and harmony, and use of rests.

MUZIO CLEMENTI

Muzio Clementi was a Classical composer, born in 1752 in Rome. This English composer of Italian birth began performing at a minor church in Rome at age fourteen, where he was "discovered" and hired by an English gentleman, Peter Beckford, to be pianist at Beckford's country house. After seven years there, he moved to London. During that time he wrote his first six piano sonatas, which brought him his first real attention. In 1780 he went on tour and played for Marie Antoinette in Paris. He then went to Vienna, where he had a famous contest with Mozart (who thought Clementi had great technique, but lacked taste as a composer). In 1785 he returned to a successful teaching and performing career in London, and from 1779 to 1790 he published about sixty piano sonatas. These had an influence on the sonatas of Beethoven. He also wrote a few symphonies. His *Gradus ad Parnassum* is a very famous set of keyboard studies, ranging from five finger pattern exercises to complicated pieces.

Clementi also enjoyed success as a businessman, investing in piano manufacturing, selling pianos, and publishing music (including some of Beethoven's works). He also did some conducting, and was one of the last to conduct from the keyboard.

After his first wife died in childbirth, Clementi remarried, and he and his second wife had four children. He retired to the country, and died in 1832.

KARL CZERNY

Karl Czerny, another Classical composer born in 1791 in Vienna, Austria, was the son of a musician. He studied with Beethoven from 1800 to 1803, and was considered one of Beethoven's finest interpreters. He began teaching at age fifteen, and from 1816 to 1823 held weekly concerts of Beethoven's music in his parents' home. He taught several famous musicians including Liszt, Thalberg, Dohler, Kullak, and Heller.

He wrote an incredible amount of music, including sacred Masses, Graduals, and Offertories, as well as symphonies, overtures, concertos, chamber music, stage works, songs, and piano sonatas. He also arranged many orchestral works of other composers (Rossini and Beethoven included) for piano duet.

Most people know Czerny mainly for his many volumes of studies and piano exercises. He also wrote the *Complete Theoretical and Practical Piano Forte School,* which gives detailed descriptions of the styles and techniques of his time. Czerny died in 1857, in Vienna.

ANTON DIABELLI

Anton Diabelli, also a Classical composer, was born in 1781 in Salzburg. This Austrian composer and music publisher studied music from an early age. In his early twenties, he moved to Vienna, and worked as a piano and guitar teacher, and as a proofreader. In 1818 he became a partner in the music publishing firm of Cappi, later to become Diabelli and Company in 1824. His company published most of Schubert's compositions.

Diabelli also did a good deal of composing, including an opera, sacred music, chamber music, piano sonatinas, and music for guitar. He is also well known for a composition which he did not write himself, but one which Beethoven composed, *33 Variations on a Waltz by Diabelli.* This work came about when Diabelli commissioned fifty composers to write one variation each on his theme. Besides Beethoven (who took the task far beyond one variation), those commissioned included Schubert, Czerny, and Liszt (who was eleven years old). Diabelli died in Vienna in 1858.

Other composers of the Classical period include:

Ludwig von Beethoven, born in Germany, 1770-1827

Franz Josef Haydn, born in Austria, 1732-1809

W.A. Mozart, born in Austria, 1756-1791

Frederich Kuhlau, born in Germany, 1786-1832

1. List the four characteristics of music from the Classical Period mentioned above, and describe each.

a. _____

b. _____

c. _____

d. _____

2. Complete the following information about each of these composers.

   a. **Muzio Clementi**

   Dates of birth and death: _____

   Historical period: _____

   Country of birth: _____

   Types of compositions: _____
   _____

   Positions held: _____
   _____
   _____

   Other contributions to music: _____
   _____

   b. **Carl Czerny**

   Dates of birth and death: _____

   Historical period: _____

   Country of birth: _____

   Positions held: _____
   _____

   Types of works: _____
   _____
   _____

   Studied with: _____

   Best known for: _____

c. **Anton Diabelli**

Dates of birth and death: _____

Historical period: _____

Country of birth: _____

Types of compositions: _____

_____

Positions held: _____

_____

_____

Composition he inspired: _____

_____

3. Name four other Classical composers, their places of birth, and their dates of birth and death.

_____ _____ _____

_____ _____ _____

_____ _____ _____

_____ _____ _____

4. Name the three sections of Sonata (or Sonata Allegro) form.

_____ _____ _____

LESSON 18
THE ROMANTIC PERIOD
FIELD, HELLER, AND MENDELSSOHN

The **ROMANTIC PERIOD** was from approximately 1830-1900. Music of the Romantic Period is the most popular of the four periods of music history. Some characteristics of this music are:

a. **Programme Music:** Much of the music of the Romantic period was written about things, people, places, or feelings. The titles in music of the period reflect the mood of the piece (such as *Curious Story* by Heller, *Blindman's Buff* by Schumann, or *Valse Melancolique* by Rebikoff).

b. **Harmonies more complicated:** Composers began to add more colorful notes to their chords, using more chromaticism, and straying from the tonal scale.

c. **Lyric melodies:** Many of the melodies in music of the Romantic period are lovely, singing melodies that have become favorites among music lovers.

d. **Rhythms more complicated:** Music of the Romantic period contains many syncopated rhythms, complicated sixteenth note patterns, dotted rhythms, triplets, cross rhythms (two against three), etc.

This example, from *Reaper's Song* by Schumann, shows these characteristics: A descriptive title, more complex chords, more complicated rhythms, lyric melody.

JOHN FIELD

John Field was an Irish pianist and composer of the Romantic Period, born in 1782 in Dublin. He was a child prodigy, and at age ten his father (a professional violinist) brought him to London to study with Clementi. By age seventeen, he had composed and performed his First Piano Concerto, and had published three piano sonatas. Besides studying with Clementi, he also travelled with him, promoting pianos and Clementi's music and publications. It was during these travels that Field chose to make Russia his home, living in Moscow and St. Petersburg.

Field was known as one of the finest pianists of his time, and was highly regarded as an improviser. He is considered the inventor of the piano nocturne, and wrote piano sonatas, concertos, fantasies, and chamber music. Field died in 1837 in Moscow.

STEPHEN HELLER

Stephen Heller, another Romantic composer, was born in Hungary in 1813. He studied music as a child from several local teachers, then went to Vienna to study with Czerny. After that he studied with Anton Halm, through whom he met Beethoven and Schubert. A two year concert tour at age fourteen caused him to have a nervous breakdown in Augsburg, where he remained for eight years to teach and compose after his recovery.

It was during his stay in Augsburg that Heller submitted some compositions to Schumann for his journal *Neue Zeitschrift für Musik.* After reviewing these, Schumann invited Heller to be the Augsburg correspondent to the journal.

Heller moved to Paris in 1838, where he worked as a critic and composer of popular music. Most of his works are for piano, and include variations, studies, character pieces, transcriptions, sonatas, sonatinas, and short pieces. He also wrote some music for violin and piano, and some early songs. Many of his works are either lost, or were never published. Heller remained in Paris until his death in 1888.

FELIX BARTHOLDY-MENDELSSOHN

Felix Bartholdy-Mendelssohn was a Romantic composer born in Hamburg, Germany in 1809. The name Bartholdy (which was taken from some family property) was added when his father, who was Jewish, converted to Christianity, and wished to distinguish the Christian branch of the family. In 1811 the family moved to Berlin. Mendelssohn was given a rigorous and complete private education which included music. He was talented in many areas, and composed several works by his mid teens. By age twenty, he had written several more compositions, including his *Overture to a Midsummer Night's Dream.*

Mendelssohn became extremely interested in the music of J.S. Bach (which had been neglected since Bach's death), and gave the first modern performance of the *Saint Matthew Passion* (for choir and orchestra) in 1829.

He went on several tours to complete his education, at which time he made many contacts that would further his career. He became quite busy as a conductor in various places, and eventually was director of a new conservatory in Leipzig. Because of his busy life, Mendelssohn had less time to compose, but he did manage to complete some chamber music, a choral symphony, incidental music to *a Midsummer Night's Dream,* his oratorio *Elijah,* and his Violin Concerto. He wrote several solo piano works, including his *Songs Without Words,* which were composed throughout his lifetime.

The hectic schedule took its toll on Mendelssohn's health, and he died in 1847 at the age of 38. His death was considered a tragedy, and the train which brought his coffin to Berlin was greeted at every stop by mourners.

Six other Romantic composers are:

Johannes Brahms, born in Germany, 1833-1897

Frederick Chopin, born in Poland, 1810-1849

Antonin Dvorak, born in Prague, 1841-1904

Edvard Grieg, born in Norway, 1843-1907

Franz Schubert, born in Austria, 1797-1828

Robert Schumann, born in Germany, 1810-1856

1. List the four characteristics of music from the Romantic Period mentioned above, and describe each.

a. _____

_____

_____

b. _____

_____

_____

c. _____

_____

_____

d. _____

_____

_____

2. Complete the following information about each of these composers.

a. **John Field**

Dates of birth and death: _____

Historical Period: _____

Country of birth: _____

Country where some of life was spent: _____

Works: _____

Relationship with Clementi: _____

b. **Stephen Heller**

Dates of birth and death: _____

Historical Period: _____

Country of birth: _____

Country where lived: _____

Studied with: _____

Positions held: _____

_____

Types of compositions: _____

_____

c. **Felix Bartholdy-Mendelssohn**

Dates of birth and death: _____

Historical Period: _____

Country of birth: _____

Relationship to Bach: _____

Positions held: _____

_____

Types of compositions: _____

_____

_____

3. Name six other Romantic composers, their places of birth, and their dates of birth and death.

_____	_____	_____
_____	_____	_____
_____	_____	_____
_____	_____	_____
_____	_____	_____
_____	_____	_____

LESSON 19
THE CONTEMPORARY PERIOD
BRITTEN, POULENC, AND STRAVINSKY

Many changes have taken place in the way music sounds during the **Contemporary Period (1900-present).** (See notes on the Contemporary Period on page 121.)

a. **Major and minor tonalities avoided**, with non-tonal (not in Major or minor keys) harmonies being used.

b. **Quartal Harmony:** The use of 4ths to make up chords, rather than thirds.

QUARTAL HARMONY

c. **Bitonality:** The use of two different keys at the same time.

BITONALITY

d. **Polytonality:** The use of many different keys at the same time.

POLYTONALITY

e. **Atonality:** No specific key used.

ATONALITY

f. **Irregular and changing meters:** Composers often use uncommon time signatures such as 5/4 or 7/4, or change the time signature during the course of the music (complex meter).

g. **Polyphonic texture:** This texture is often used, with the harmonies becoming the result of the entangling of the melodic lines.

h. **Neo-Classic writing:** Composers often write Sonatas, Sonatinas, or other forms which were common during the Classical Period.

This example, from *Evening in the Country* by Bartok, shows these characteristics: polyphonic texture, changing (complex) meter, avoidance of Major and minor tonalities.

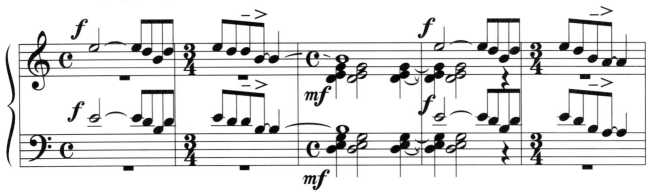

BENJAMIN BRITTEN

Benjamin Britten was a Contemporary composer, pianist, and conductor. Britten was born in 1913 in England, and was the youngest of four children. His father was a dentist, and his mother was musical. He began piano at age five, at which age he also began composing. A few years later, he studied composition with Frank Bridge. He attended the Royal College beginning in 1930, where he wrote several compositions which were performed in London. He wrote music for a documentary film company and theatre music, and many of his other works were played at various festivals.

After this time, Britten began writing many large-scale works, and had an illustrious career composing operas, song cycles, concertos, and other works. His most famous works are the opera *Peter Grimes,* and his *War Requiem* for choir and orchestra. Although Britten was a Contemporary composer, he wrote in a relatively conservative style compared with his contemporaries. His music was, however, influenced by his political views (he was a pacifist). Britten died in 1976.

FRANCIS POULENC

Francis Poulenc was a Contemporary French composer, born in Paris in 1899. Although he did study piano with Ricardo Vines, he was a self-taught composer. Much of his music shows a witty, anti-conventional style. He was part of the 20th Century French circle of composers called *Les Six,* which also included Auric, Durey, Honneger, Milhaud, and Tailleferre, whose philosophy was that music should be sparce, up to date, and witty.

Poulenc wrote a variety of music, including song cycles, concertos, and operas. He is also well known for his sacred choral works, which include the unaccompanied *Mass,* and the *Stabat Mater* and *Gloria,* both for soprano, choir, and orchestra. Poulenc died in Paris in 1963.

IGOR STRAVINSKY

Igor Stravinsky was also a Contemporary composer, born in 1882 in Russia. Stravinsky's father was a bass in the Imperial Opera, and he studied piano and composition as a young boy. He studied with Rimsky-Korsakov from 1903 to 1906. In 1910, at age 28, he went to Paris with a ballet company, and began writing a series of ballets for the troupe. The first was the *Firebird,* followed by *Petrushka,* then *The Rite of Spring,* which would become his most famous work. Its driving rhythms, syncopations, and changing meters made this dramatic work a turning point in 20th century compositional techniques. Stravinsky wrote in neo-classic style, the use of Classical forms (and those of other periods), combined with 20th Century rhythms and harmonies.

Stravinsky remained in Paris until the early 1940's, when he moved to Los Angeles. He continued writing in his neo-classic style until the early 1950's, when he began exploring serial or twelve-tone writing (a method of composition which uses all twelve tones of the chromatic scale, not randomly, but within strict guidelines).

Besides the many ballets, he made use of other forms, including opera, concerto, Mass, cantata, and orchestral forms. Stravinsky remained in Los Angeles until his death in 1971.

Six other Contemporary composers include:

Bela Bartok, born in Hungary, 1881-1945

Aaron Copland, born in U.S.A., 1900-1990

Norman Della-Joio, born in U.S.A., 1913-

Dmitri Kabalevsky, born in Russia, 1904-1987

Sergei Prokofiev, born in Russia, 1891-1953

Dmitri Shostakovich, born in Russia, 1906-1975

1. List the eight characteristics of music from the Contemporary Period mentioned above, and describe each.

   a. _____

   b. _____

   c. _____

   d. _____

   e. _____

   f. _____

   g. _____

   h. _____

2. Complete the following information about each of these composers.

a. Benjamin Britten

Dates of birth and death: _____

Historical Period: _____

Country of birth: _____

Education: _____

Positions held: _____

Compositions: _____

Style: _____

b. **Francis Poulenc**

Dates of birth and death: _____

Historical Period: _____

Country of birth: _____

Education: _____

Style of writing: _____

_____

Types of compositions: _____

_____

Les Six (names of composers, and style): _____

_____

_____

c. **Igor Stravinsky**

Dates of birth and death: _____

Historical Period: _____

Country of birth: _____

Education: _____

Early style of writing: _____

_____

Later style of writing: _____

_____

Types of compositions: _____

_____

3. Name six other Contemporary composers, their places of birth, and their dates of birth and death.

_____ _____ _____
_____ _____ _____
_____ _____ _____
_____ _____ _____
_____ _____ _____
_____ _____ _____

REVIEW
LESSONS 11-19

1. Write the counts for these phrases, and place accents on the strong beats.

a. From *Invention No. 6* by J.S. Bach.

b. From *Mazurka, Op. 67, No. 4,* by Chopin.

c. From *Sonata, Op. 49, No. 1,* by Beethoven.

2. Define these terms.

a. Atonality _____

b. Bitonality _____

c. Canon _____

d. Enharmonic _____

e. Parallel Major and minor _____

f. Polytonality _____

g. Relative Major and minor _____

h. ritenuto _____

i. scherzando _____

j. syncopation _____

k. m.d. _____

l. m.s. _____

3. Circle the compositional technique used in each of these examples (repetition, sequence, imitation, pedal point, canon, augmentation, or diminution), and write the type of technique on the line above the music.

a. From *Little Fugue* by Schumann. _____

b. From *Invention No. 3* by J.S. Bach. _____

c. Original. _____

d. From *Song of War* by Schumann. _____

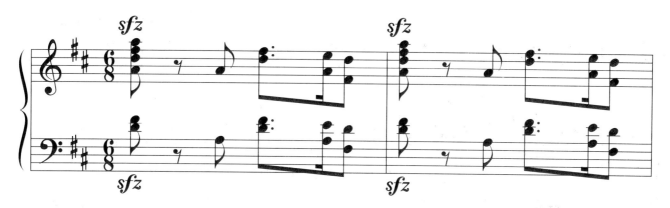

e. From *Little Fugue* by Schumann. _____

f. Original. _____

4. Name the texture used in each of the following examples.

a. From *Little Fugue* by Schumann. _____

b. From *Song of War* by Schumann. _____

5. Match the following occurences in music history with the appropriate period.

   a. Baroque   b. Classical   c. Romantic   d. Contemporary

   _____ Use of ornamentation
   _____ Sonata and Sonatina forms developed
   _____ Irregular and changing meters
   _____ Lyric melodies
   _____ Homophonic texture predominates
   _____ Programme music
   _____ Polyphonic texture in which harmonies are determined by the combinations of each individual line
   _____ Neo-classic style
   _____ Dance suites
   _____ Terraced dynamics
   _____ Harmonic structure and cadence points clearly defined
   _____ Atonality, Bitonality, and Polytonality
   _____ Colorful harmonies (within Major and minor tonalities)
   _____ Polyphonic texture (within Major and minor tonalities)
   _____ Alberti bass

6. Name the three sections of Sonata Allegro form.

   _____   _____   _____

7. Define **meter.** _____

8. Give the period, dates, and three important facts about the lives of these composers.

Benjamin Britten:

Muzio Clementi:

John Field:

Johann Philipp Kirnberger:

Carl Czerny:

Francis Poulenc:

Felix Bartholdy-Mendelssohn:

Antonio Vivaldi:

Anton Diabelli:

Stephen Heller:

Igor Stravinsky:

Georg Philipp Telemann:

9. Transpose this excerpt (from *Sonatina, Op. 36, No. 1,* by Clementi) to the key of A Major. Write the transposition on the blank staff below the example.

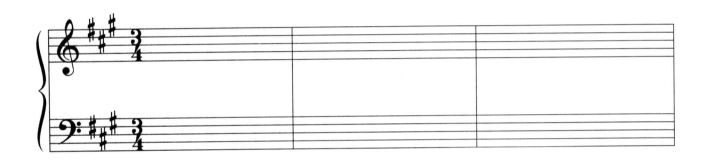

Score: _____ **REVIEW TEST** Perfect Score: 90
Passing Score: 63

1. Match the type of scale used in each of the following examples with its name. (6 points)

    _____ Major   _____ Chromatic   _____ melodic minor

    _____ Whole tone   _____ harmonic minor   _____ natural minor

2. Name the Major key to which each of the following Dominant 7th chords belongs. (6 points)

_____   _____   _____   _____   _____   _____

3. A theme is given below. The theme has been changed in the next two examples. Give the name of each compositional technique used. (2 points)

Example A: _____

Example B: _____

4. Write the counts for the following rhythm. (5 points)

5. Match the following techniques with the appropriate period of music history. (4 points)

    a. Baroque   _____ Bitonality/Polytonality

    b. Classical   _____ Programme music

    c. Romantic   _____ Sonata form

    d. Contemporary   _____ Dance Suite

6. Match these composers with their periods. (8 points)

   a. Baroque   _____ Clementi
                         _____ Field
   b. Classical   _____ Kirnberger
                         _____ Poulenc
   c. Romantic   _____ Czerny
                         _____ Stravinsky
   d. Contemporary   _____ Vivaldi
                         _____ Mendelssohn

7. Label these secondary dominants. Use the Major key for each example. (The first one is given.) (5 points)

   (V^7 of IV) IV _____ _____ _____ _____ _____

8. Match the following terms with their definitions.

   a. Polyphonic texture   _____ Dominant to Submediant

   b. Modulation   _____ Doubling of note values

   c. Deceptive cadence   _____ Two or more voices of equal importance

   d. scherzando   _____ Playfully

   e. Augmentation   _____ Strong notes on weak beats

   f. Syncopation   _____ Change of key

9. The following example is from *Invention No. 15* by J.S. Bach. Answer the questions about the music. (12 points)

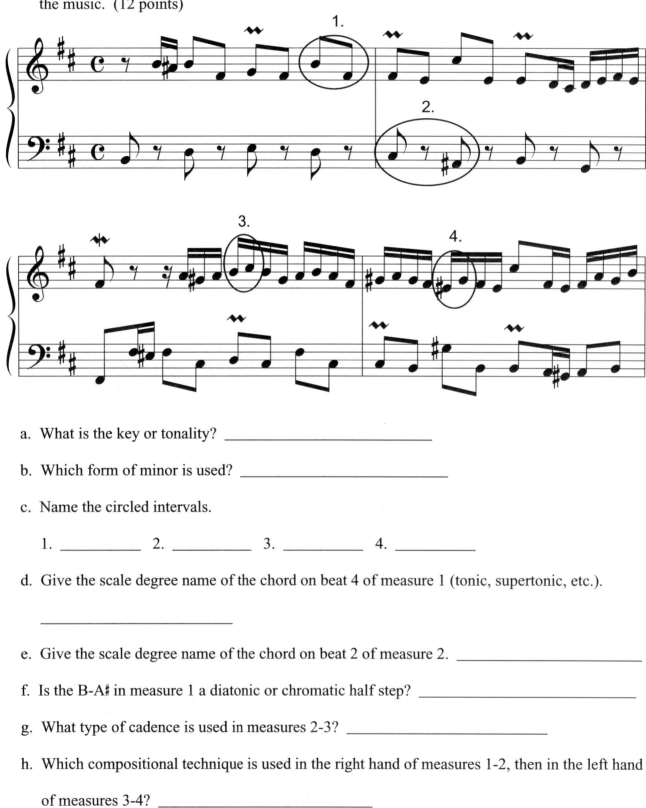

a. What is the key or tonality? _____

b. Which form of minor is used? _____

c. Name the circled intervals.

   1. _____   2. _____   3. _____   4. _____

d. Give the scale degree name of the chord on beat 4 of measure 1 (tonic, supertonic, etc.).

   _____

e. Give the scale degree name of the chord on beat 2 of measure 2. _____

f. Is the B-A♯ in measure 1 a diatonic or chromatic half step? _____

g. What type of cadence is used in measures 2-3? _____

h. Which compositional technique is used in the right hand of measures 1-2, then in the left hand of measures 3-4? _____

i. Which period of music history does J.S. Bach represent? _____

10. The following example is from *Sonata, K. 280,* by Mozart. Answer the questions about the music. (12 points)

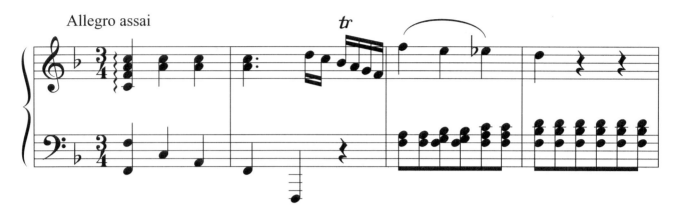

a. What is the key or tonality? _____

b. Give the scale degree names of the chords outlined in the following measures:

   Measure 1: _____   Measure 4: _____   Measure 6: _____

c. What type of half step is the E-E♭ in measure 3? _____

d. What type of rhythmic device is used in measure 8, treble clef? _____

e. Name the ornament used in measure 2. _____

   Circle the correct way to play this ornament.

f. Give the meaning of *Allegro assai.* _____

g. Which period of music does Mozart represent? _____

h. Name two other composers from this same period. _____   _____

11. The following example is from *Nocturne* by Grieg. Answer the questions about the music. (12 points)

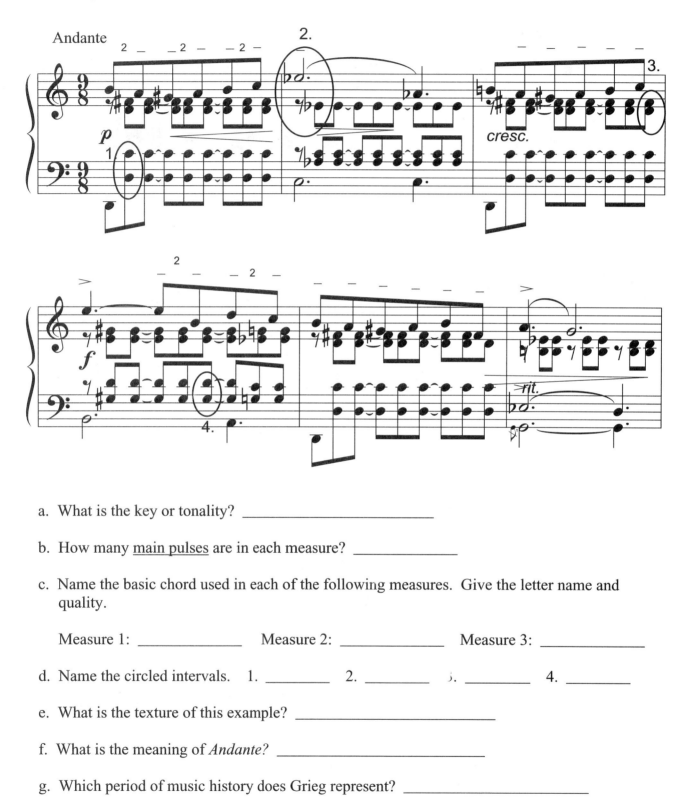

a. What is the key or tonality? _____

b. How many <u>main pulses</u> are in each measure? _____

c. Name the basic chord used in each of the following measures. Give the letter name and quality.

   Measure 1: _____   Measure 2: _____   Measure 3: _____

d. Name the circled intervals. 1. _____ 2. _____ 3. _____ 4. _____

e. What is the texture of this example? _____

f. What is the meaning of *Andante*? _____

g. Which period of music history does Grieg represent? _____

12. The following example is from *Three Rondos* by Bartok. Answer the questions about the music. (12 points)

a. What is the key at the beginning of the example? _____

b. What is the key after the double bar? _____

c. What term is used for a change of key? _____

d. What is the meaning of *Allegro giocoso*? _____

e. What is the meaning of *ritenuto molto*? _____

f. Give the letter name and quality of the basic chords in each of the following measures.

   Measure 2: _____   Measure 5: _____   Measure 8, beat 1: _____

g. What would the time signature be? _____'

h. Which period of music does Bartok represent? _____

i. Name two other composers from this same period. _____ _____

REFERENCES

Apel, Willi. *Harvard Dictionary of Music, Second Edition.* Cambridge, Massachussetts: Belknap Press of Harvard University Press, 1972.

Arnold, Denis, ed. *The New Oxford Companion to Music, Volumes 1 and 2.* New York: Oxford University Press, 1983.

Music Teachers' Association of California. *Certificate of Merit Piano Syllabus.* San Francisco: Music Teachers' Association of California, 1992.

Music Teachers' Association of California. *Certificate of Merit Piano Syllabus.* Ontario, Canada: Frederick Harris Music Co., Limited, 1997.

Music Teachers' Association of California. *Certificate of Merit Piano Syllabus.* San Francisco: Music Teachers' Association of California, 2007.

Russell, John. *A History of Music for Young People.* Toronto, Canada: Clark, Irwin & Company Limited, 1965.

Sadie, Stanley, ed. *The New Grove Dictionary of Music and Musicians.* Washington, D.C.: Grove's Dictionaries of Music Inc., 1980.

BASICS OF KEYBOARD THEORY

Workbooks by Julie McIntosh Johnson
Computer Activities by Nancy Plourde

```
NAME    _____
ADDRESS _____
CITY _____ STATE _____ ZIP _____
PHONE _____ E-MAIL _____
```

QTY	ITEM	COST	TOTAL
	PREPARATORY LEVEL	9.50	
	LEVEL 1	9.50	
	LEVEL 2	9.50	
	LEVEL 3	9.95	
	LEVEL 4	9.95	
	LEVEL 5	10.50	
	LEVEL 6	10.50	
	LEVEL 7	10.95	
	LEVEL 8	11.95	
	LEVEL 9	12.95	
	Level 10 (Advanced)	12.50	
	ANSWER BOOK	11.95	
	COMPUTER ACTIVITIES LEVELS PREP-2, Mac/PC	49.95	
	COMPUTER ACTIVITIES LEVELS 3-4, Mac/PC	39.95	
	COMPUTER ACTIVITIES LEVELS 5-6, PC Only	49.95	

Shipping:
 1-5 Books.........$5.00
 6-10 Books.......$6.00
 11 or more........$7.00

Sub-Total	
Calif. Residents: Sales Tax	
Shipping	
TOTAL	

Make checks payable to:
J. Johnson Music Publications
5062 Siesta Lane
Yorba Linda, CA 92886
714-961-0257   www.bktmusic.com   info@bktmusic.com